Mitigating Challenges to U.S.-Russia Strategic Stability

SAMUEL CHARAP, JOHN DRENNAN, LUKE GRIFFITH,
EDWARD GEIST, BRIAN G. CARLSON

Prepared for the Defense Threat Reduction Agency
Approved for public release; distribution unlimited

NATIONAL DEFENSE RESEARCH INSTITUTE

For more information on this publication, visit **www.rand.org/t/RRA1094-1**.

About RAND

The RAND Corporation is a research organization that develops solutions to public policy challenges to help make communities throughout the world safer and more secure, healthier and more prosperous. RAND is nonprofit, nonpartisan, and committed to the public interest. To learn more about RAND, visit www.rand.org.

Research Integrity

Our mission to help improve policy and decisionmaking through research and analysis is enabled through our core values of quality and objectivity and our unwavering commitment to the highest level of integrity and ethical behavior. To help ensure our research and analysis are rigorous, objective, and nonpartisan, we subject our research publications to a robust and exacting quality-assurance process; avoid both the appearance and reality of financial and other conflicts of interest through staff training, project screening, and a policy of mandatory disclosure; and pursue transparency in our research engagements through our commitment to the open publication of our research findings and recommendations, disclosure of the source of funding of published research, and policies to ensure intellectual independence. For more information, visit www.rand.org/about/principles.

RAND's publications do not necessarily reflect the opinions of its research clients and sponsors.

Published by the RAND Corporation, Santa Monica, Calif.
© 2022 RAND Corporation
RAND® is a registered trademark.

Library of Congress Cataloging-in-Publication Data is available for this publication.
ISBN: 978-1-9774-0705-4

About This Report

This report documents research and analysis conducted as part of a project entitled *Rethinking U.S.-Russia Strategic Deterrence*. The purpose of the project was to analyze the military, technological, and other strategic dynamics that are eroding the viability of the U.S.-Russia strategic deterrence paradigm and to identify potential policy options to address this challenge. The objective was to investigate possible alternative paradigms that can meet the requirement of sustaining mutual deterrence—both today and in the future—and address the downsides associated with the status quo.

The research reported here was completed in May 2021 and underwent security review with the sponsor and the Defense Office of Prepublication and Security Review before public release.

RAND National Security Research Division

This research was sponsored by the Defense Threat Reduction Agency and conducted within the International Security and Defense Policy (ISDP) Center of the RAND National Security Research Division (NSRD), which operates the National Defense Research Institute (NDRI), a federally funded research and development center sponsored by the Office of the Secretary of Defense, the Joint Staff, the Unified Combatant Commands, the Navy, the Marine Corps, the defense agencies, and the defense intelligence enterprise.

For more information on the RAND ISDP Center, see www.rand.org/nsrd/isdp or contact the director (contact information is provided on the webpage).

Acknowledgments

The authors would like to thank the Defense Threat Reduction Agency's Strategic Trends Division for sponsoring the project. Specifically, we are grateful to Jennifer Perry, Research Program Coordinator, for her support, understanding, and interest in making this project a success. She and her colleagues provided important input at several stages.

We would also like to thank our colleague Lt Gen (Ret.) Frank Klotz at the RAND Corporation and Heather Williams of the Massachusetts Institute of Technology and King's College London, whose reviews of this report challenged our thinking in positive ways and greatly improved the final product.

Summary

The U.S.-Russian bilateral stability paradigm rests on the shared confidence that one side's preemptive counterforce strike would fail to disarm the other. Both sides are mutually vulnerable to retaliation and thus have no incentive to strike first. Nonetheless, the United States has developed significant prompt counterforce capabilities that Moscow fears could be used for a first strike. These threat perceptions have become a significant source of instability.

A variety of developments relating to the sides' nuclear forces and their other strategic capabilities has led in recent years to an asymmetry of perceived vulnerability to preemption. The United States has pointed to certain Russian activities in the strategic domain that Washington considers problematic or even destabilizing, but Washington has not raised concerns that Moscow could undermine U.S. retaliatory capability. Indeed, Russia cannot plausibly threaten the lion's share of U.S. strategic forces with a counterforce strike; moreover, evidence suggests that Moscow is not developing capabilities that could hold most U.S. forces at risk. Although the United States lacks the ability to deliver a decisive disarming blow, it does maintain far greater counterforce capabilities and leaves open the possibility of using its strategic forces for damage limitation strikes. Furthermore, the United States continues to develop related strategic capabilities, such as ballistic missile defenses (BMDs) and long-range conventional strike, that Moscow believes could be used in concert with a counterforce nuclear strike to blunt Russia's deterrent.

In this report, we examine the historical origins of the divergence in approaches that created this asymmetry, analyze resulting Russian threat perceptions, assess the pluses and minuses associated with current U.S. policy, and evaluate alternative approaches that could improve strategic stability.

In the United States, counterforce targeting began in the 1960s as a consideration for retaliation. The shift away from an exclusive emphasis on counterforce retaliation and the development of capabilities to target much of the Soviet arsenal were driven by the need to maintain damage limitation options and ensure the credibility of U.S. extended deterrence while accounting for the 1970s growth in Soviet nuclear forces and the conventional imbalance in Europe. The United States has maintained significant counterforce capabilities and the ability to deliver them promptly ever since. The end of the Cold War, the collapse of the Soviet Union, and the dramatic reductions in nuclear forces achieved through strategic arms control never shook the U.S. commitment to maintaining a formidable prompt counterforce capability.

After the 1960s, Soviet—and, later, Russian—nuclear strategy did not prioritize capabilities for a credible counterforce option. Instead, the requirement to inflict *unacceptable damage* even after Russian forces have been degraded by a first strike was the core requirement for effective deterrence. Instead of trying to match U.S. capabilities quantitatively or qualitatively, the Soviet Union would field weapons sufficient to ensure that the United States would never escape unacceptable damage irrespective of its investments in offensive weapons and missile defenses. Whereas the U.S. concept of assured destruction was a measure of sufficiency distinct from employment policy, Soviet and Russian military writings suggest that their nuclear war plans were *designed* to subject an attacker to unacceptable damage with retaliatory strikes.

In short, for largely historically contingent reasons, the U.S. strategic force has significant counterforce capability and its employment policy openly discusses damage limitation, while the Russian emphasis is on ensuring enough retaliation to effect unacceptable damage.

Although the exact number of warheads that the Russian military has specified as necessary for ensuring unacceptable damage in retaliation remains unknown, it is clear that the requirements for a retaliatory strike are significant. Since the 1990s, Russian strategists have fretted about their country's ability to fulfill those requirements. One group calculated that, whereas the United States was able to deliver only one warhead on each Soviet intercontinental ballistic missile in 1991, that number had tripled by 1999 because of the changes in the sides' capabilities. In addition to the relative decline in Russia's strategic nuclear forces, Moscow's confidence in its ability to ensure retaliation has been steadily eroding over the course of the post-Soviet period for several additional reasons. Russia's concern is that a combination of new U.S. capabilities—which include conventional precision-guided missiles, BMDs, and cyber and space capabilities—and the qualitative superiority of the U.S. nuclear triad itself could eventually provide the United States with a viable option for a disarming first strike.

There are four major consequences for the United States of Russia's growing concern about its ability to retaliate after a counterforce first strike. First, Moscow has developed a suite of novel capabilities to address this concern. Second, Russia seems unwilling to reduce its strategic nuclear forces below New START levels as a result of the heightened requirements to ensure unacceptable damage in retaliation.[1] Third, the overall stability of the bilateral relationship, and thus its ability to deliver on U.S. national interests, has eroded, in no small part because of divergences over strategic issues. Many in Moscow seem convinced that geopolitical blackmail using the threat of a disarming strike is possible at some point in the future. Therefore, Russia's concerns about preemption are relevant not only in a crisis but also during what the United States would consider a peacetime context. Fourth, and finally, a strong case can be made that Russian concerns about preemption might incentivize a first strike in a serious crisis. The United States has an interest in ensuring that Russia is not driven to initiate a strategic exchange over use-them-or-lose-them concerns.

---

[1] New START (strategic arms reduction treaty) is used to refer to the Treaty Between the United States and the Russian Federation on Measures for the Further Reduction and Limitation of Strategic Offensive Arms, signed on April 8, 2010.

These four negative consequences should be weighed against five significant benefits provided by current U.S. posture: effective deterrence, damage limitation, hedging, arms control, and international legality. This report describes each in greater detail. Although it is clear that the current approach does provide for these benefits, it is not clear that this approach is *required* to obtain them. None of the five is a binary value; some *degree* of each might be achieved under a different approach.

In this report, we analyze three categories of possible policy changes that could address Russian concerns about preemption: a paradigm shift in U.S. nuclear policy, mutually negotiated structural transformations (i.e., significant changes to nuclear capabilities), and negotiated mutual self-restraint measures. A paradigm shift would entail addressing preemption concerns directly by changing U.S. nuclear policy fundamentally. Structural transformations in the U.S. and Russian arsenals could rule out or significantly complicate counterforce strikes by modifying capabilities. Self-restraint measures are more-modest steps that reduce preemption concerns but do not require dramatic changes in policies or capabilities.

A paradigm shift in U.S. nuclear policy could significantly mitigate and perhaps even completely resolve the instability created by Russian preemption concerns. However, some experts counter that doing so would imperil U.S. and allied security by weakening deterrence. Unless negotiated with Russia in return for significant concessions, such an approach seems unlikely to be politically viable in the United States and could call into question the need for arms control, which is a stabilizing force in the relationship. Given the present configuration of the U.S. and Russian arsenals, neither of the two possible structural transformations evaluated in the report would seem a practical way forward to address Russian preemption concerns.

Although a paradigm shift would be required to *eliminate* the destabilizing effect of Russian preemption concerns completely, there are measures that the United States and Russia could take either together or unilaterally but in coordination that could reduce concerns about preemption without radically changing U.S. nuclear policy. These measures, summarized in Table S.1, would provide a degree of reassurance about the parties' lack of intention to execute a preemp-

Table S.1
Self-Restraint Measures

Measure	Description
Increased transparency of nuclear-powered ballistic missile submarines (SSBNs) through exchange of maintenance schedules	Regular exchange of maintenance schedules to provide more predictability about the actual number of operational submarine-launched ballistic missiles (SLBMs) deployed and reduce uncertainty about the size of a possible U.S. strike
Commitments not to operate SSBNs in certain areas	U.S. commitment not to conduct SSBN operations near the Russian coast to ensure a minimum time of flight for SLBM launches and thus provide assurance regarding warning time; Russian commitment not to operate SSBNs outside their bastions
Ban on depressed trajectory flight tests of SLBMs	Mutual agreement to ban depressed trajectory launches—as neither side has conducted them or indicated an intention to do so—to mitigate preemption fears
Ban on deployment of space-to-Earth weapons	Specific commitment not to deploy weapons that could strike earthbound targets from space—separately from those weapons, such as antisatellite weapons, that are currently the subject of a broader debate between the United States and Russia (and other countries) over the militarization of space
Ban or limit on ground-based and/or air-based deployments of prompt conventional strike options in proximity to borders	Bilaterally negotiated ban or unilaterally declared limits on ground-based deployments of intermediate- and medium-range cruise or ballistic missiles to limit both decapitation concerns for Russia and nuclear decoupling concerns for the North Atlantic Treaty Organization
Commitment not to strike nuclear command, control, and communication (NC3) and early-warning assets in a conventional conflict	Commitment not to strike NC3 and early-warning assets in the context of a conventional conflict to attempt to mitigate some use-them-or-lose-them concerns without sacrificing any operational requirements
Commitment not to operate attack submarines near Russian SSBN bastions or U.S. coasts	Limitation on how close U.S. and Russian attack submarines can operate near SSBN bases to reduce concerns about survivability
Commitment to provide advance notification of increased bomber alert status	Commitment not to put bombers on alert except during training exercises and to notify the other side of those exercises well in advance
Self-restraint commitments on BMDs	Adjustable and voluntary commitment to provide the other side with annual accounts of inventory of BMD interceptors, launchers, and associated radars and a ten-year plan for any increases in that inventory, along with a commitment to provide advance notification of any change in those plans

tive counterforce strike by complicating the ability to carry out such a strike on short notice.

In addition to negotiating such measures, U.S. policymakers could take the initiative by proposing a bilateral dialogue that systematically examines the issues that raise Russian concerns about preemption.

These modest changes could mitigate the negative consequences of the current approach without any dramatic changes in force structure, posture, or even employment policy. The United States would maintain essentially all of the five benefits associated with the status quo. The stabilizing benefits of these steps, however, could be significant.

Contents

Tables

CHAPTER ONE

Introduction

As they did during most of the Cold War, both Washington and Moscow define *stability* in the bilateral deterrence relationship as confidence in the ability to impose unacceptable damage on the other side even if it attempts a disarming first strike. This confidence creates *first-strike or crisis stability*; i.e., neither side has an incentive to use (or threaten to use) nuclear weapons first because both know that any attempt to disarm the other would fail. Thus, the consequences of such an attempt would be unacceptable. The state of mutually assured destruction, reinforced by treaty-based limitations, also disincentivizes arms racing. This dual definition of stability—crisis stability and arms-race stability—was implicit in a U.S.-Soviet 1990 joint statement, when the sides agreed to seek "agreements that improve survivability, remove incentives for a nuclear first strike and implement an appropriate relationship between strategic offenses and defenses."[1]

During the Cold War, both superpowers remained ambivalent at best about this mutual vulnerability, yet it became central to arms control and broader efforts to manage the U.S.-Soviet competition. Today, Russia and the United States continue to devote significant resources to ensuring that their retaliatory capability remains viable even after a preemptive strike.

Although this stability paradigm rests on the shared confidence that one side's preemptive counterforce strike would fail to disarm the

---

[1] United States and Soviet Union, Soviet-United States Joint Statement on Future Negotiations on Nuclear and Space Arms and Further Enhancing Strategic Stability, June 1, 1990, George H. W. Bush Presidential Library website, undated.

other, both sides—but particularly the United States—have developed significant counterforce capabilities.[2] Guaranteeing the survivability of a large portion of its strategic forces has always been a core driver of procurement and posture, but the United States has also prioritized having the ability to hold at risk much of Moscow's strategic arsenal. As we will describe in greater detail, there were many factors that drove the decisions to develop and continually improve these capabilities over the course of nearly half a century. Regardless of Washington's motives, Moscow has long viewed these capabilities, particularly when taken together with other U.S. strategic capabilities (such as missile defense), as indicative of a desire to break out of the nuclear stalemate and develop a *preemptive counterforce* option. These threat perceptions have become a significant source of instability in recent years.

Despite nominal numerical parity, the U.S.-Russia dyad has become increasingly unbalanced. A variety of developments relating to the sides' nuclear forces and their other strategic capabilities has resulted in an asymmetry of perceived vulnerability to preemption. The United States has pointed to certain Russian activities in the strategic domain that Washington considers problematic or even destabilizing, but Washington has not raised concerns that Moscow could undermine its retaliatory capability. Indeed, Russia cannot plausibly threaten the lion's share of U.S. strategic forces with a counterforce strike; moreover, the evidence suggests that Moscow is not developing capabilities that could hold most U.S. forces at risk. Although the United States lacks the ability to deliver a "splendid [disarming] first strike,"[3] it does maintain far greater counterforce capabilities and leaves open the possibility of using its strategic forces for damage limitation strikes. Furthermore, the United States continues to develop related strategic capabilities, such as (limited) ballistic missile defenses (BMDs) and long-range

---

[2]   For more on recent developments, see Keir A. Lieber and Daryl G. Press, "The New Era of Counterforce: Technological Change and the Future of Nuclear Deterrence," *International Security*, Vol. 41, No. 4, Spring 2017.

[3]   Hermann Kahn, *On Thermonuclear War*, Princeton, NJ: Princeton University Press, 1960, p. 36.

conventional strike, that Moscow fears could be used in concert with a counterforce nuclear strike to prevent an effective retaliation.

As a result, Russia's confidence in its ability to ensure that it can launch a retaliatory strike that creates unacceptable damage has slipped. Moscow sees each advancement in U.S. strategic capabilities—e.g., increased warhead accuracy, advances in BMDs, the potential for conventional prompt global strike, or advanced U.S. cyber capabilities—as steps toward an eventual U.S. ability to neutralize Russia's strategic forces without significant risk of unacceptable retaliation. The fear in Moscow is that this could allow the United States to achieve strategic dominance during a potential conflict or to engage in nuclear blackmail during peacetime to achieve geopolitical goals.

Moscow's increasing concerns about its ability to guarantee retaliation have had direct consequences for U.S. national security. First, there are increasing signs of arms race instability, albeit in ways that differ from the Cold War–era dynamic. Instead, Moscow is pursuing niche capabilities, such as a long-range autonomous nuclear torpedo, which is a doomsday device only necessary if all of the traditional legs of the Russian triad are neutralized, designed to ensure retaliation even under an extreme worst-case preemptive counterforce strike on its strategic capabilities.[4] Second, Russia seems unwilling to reduce its strategic nuclear forces below the levels established by New START as a result of its concerns about meeting requirements for ensuring enough retaliation.[5] Third, the overall stability of the bilateral relationship, and thus its ability to deliver on U.S. national interests, has eroded in no small part as a result of divergences over strategic issues. Finally, in a crisis today, Moscow's use-them-or-lose-them concerns could undermine strategic restraint. These problems are likely to become more acute over time.

---

[4]   Edward Geist and Dara Massicot, "Understanding Putin's Nuclear 'Superweapons,'" *SAIS Review of International Affairs*, Vol. 39, No. 2, 2019.

[5]   New START (strategic arms reduction treaty) is used to refer to the Treaty Between the United States and the Russian Federation on Measures for the Further Reduction and Limitation of Strategic Offensive Arms, signed on April 8, 2010.

But these challenges must be weighed against the benefits provided to the United States by its policies. In this report, we identify five core benefits and describe them in greater detail: effective deterrence, the ability to limit the damage to the United States of a Russian strike, a robust hedge against future technological or geopolitical developments, arms control agreements, and international legality of targeting policy. We therefore assess possible changes in policy that would reduce Russia's perception of vulnerability to preemption (and thus stabilize the strategic relationship) in terms of the extent to which such changes could undermine these benefits.

Research Questions

This project sought to answer the following core research questions:

- What are the origins of the current divergence in U.S. and Russian threat perceptions regarding preemption?
- What are the practical consequences of Russia's threat perceptions for U.S. interests?
- Could changes to current policies address Russian concerns while delivering the benefits afforded the United States by the status quo?

Research Approach

To answer these questions, we employed a multimethod research design. We reviewed and analyzed published materials on three central issues. First, we reviewed the extensive secondary literature on the history of U.S. and Soviet/Russian nuclear policy. (Because of resource limitations, we could not conduct original historical research.) We used relevant historical, memoir, archival, and scholarly works in English and Russian to document the evolution of targeting policy from the 1960s to the present. This historical overview allows for a better understanding of the origins of current U.S. and Russian policies and threat perceptions. Second, we analyzed a variety of Russian-language sources, including several books and journal articles written by current and former military officers, weapon-lab scientists, and defense policymakers, as well as the secondary Russian and Western scholarly literature, to document and analyze Moscow's current threat perceptions. Third, we cataloged published proposals made by experts in both countries to change U.S. and Russian strategic policies, along with various critiques of those proposals. We assessed this catalog in our own presentation of options for policy changes.

To supplement these literature reviews, we conducted interviews in Moscow in November 2019 with Russian experts, former officials, and scholars of strategic stability. We used these meetings to probe Russian threat perceptions, explore possible policy changes, and assess Moscow's openness to them. These semistructured interviews were conducted on a not-for-attribution basis. Additionally, we conducted a workshop in Washington, D.C., in January 2020 with scholars of nuclear weapon policy, former senior U.S. government officials, and retired military officers. The workshop allowed us to engage in a more nuanced discussion about challenges to bilateral strategic stability and hear different perspectives on these challenges from former practitioners. The workshop was conducted on a not-for-attribution basis.

Report Structure

This report proceeds as follows. Chapter Two briefly describes the history of U.S. and Soviet/Russian approaches to nuclear strategy as that history relates to the development of the counterforce mission for nuclear weapons and concerns about preemption. This background provides crucial context for understanding current policy challenges. Chapter Three outlines Moscow's concerns about preemption and the consequences for bilateral stability. Chapter Four addresses the key benefits provided by U.S. policies. Chapter Five reviews possible changes to those policies and assesses the extent to which those changes could deliver the benefits of the status quo while addressing the instability created by Russian preemption concerns. We offer conclusions in Chapter Six.

CHAPTER TWO

A Brief History

The U.S. strategic community has debated targeting doctrine and the potential for preemption since the advent of nuclear weapons.[1] A variety of considerations have come into play. Ethical and international legal concerns have been raised about the prospect of deliberately targeting cities and other population centers. The credibility of a deterrence strategy that depended on killing tens of millions of civilians has been called into question. Avoiding the instability associated with the possibility of preemption has remained a prominent concern in terms of both targeting and force structure. In addition to the requirement of deterring attacks on the homeland, U.S. targeting doctrine had the requirement of meeting extended deterrence commitments.

Amid these debates, the United States had by the 1970s developed significant counterforce capabilities that could threaten much of the Soviet arsenal and could be delivered promptly. U.S. capability developments and embrace of damage limitation led the Soviets to fear a preemptive first strike on their forces. Despite the end of the Cold War, and even as the overall number of nuclear weapons has been dramatically reduced, U.S. counterforce capabilities have been maintained—some have argued that they have even been enhanced.

By the time it had hardened its intercontinental ballistic missile (ICBM) silos and fielded the first nuclear-powered ballistic missile submarines (SSBNs) in 1961, the United States was largely confident in its ability to retaliate with large numbers of warheads after any Soviet

---

[1] See Lawrence Freedman and Jeffrey Michaels, *The Evolution of Nuclear Strategy*, 4th ed., New York: Palgrave Macmillan, 2019.

attack (although Washington devoted vast resources to keep up its confidence in subsequent decades). By contrast, nuclear strategists in Moscow have focused since the 1970s on the task of effecting *unacceptable damage* in retaliation after an attempted disarming first strike and worried that their forces were inadequate for achieving that objective. This worry drove a Soviet and, later, Russian focus on ensuring enough retaliation to deter a U.S. first strike while largely abandoning aspirations for an effective counterforce strike option. This chapter briefly describes the historical roots of this divergence in approaches and threat perceptions. This overview lays the groundwork for a more fulsome discussion of current dynamics in the subsequent chapters.

The Development of U.S. Counterforce Doctrine and Capabilities

Counterforce and the Cold War

Speaking to the North Atlantic Council in Athens, Greece, on May 5, 1962, Secretary of Defense Robert McNamara announced the end of the Eisenhower administration's strategy of massive retaliation. Part of the so-called New Look, massive retaliation prescribed an all-out nuclear strike on Soviet urban and industrial centers in response to a Soviet first strike.[2] The Kennedy administration's strategy of flexible response, by contrast, called for symmetrical, graduated retaliation against potential Soviet aggression. At the North Atlantic Council meeting, McNamara unveiled the counterforce/no cities doctrine, a facet of flexible response. In a nuclear conflict, "our principal military objectives . . . should be the destruction of the enemy's military forces while attempting to preserve" U.S. and "allied society," he declared. "If both sides were to confine their attacks to important military targets,

---

[2] John Gaddis, *Strategies of Containment: A Critical Appraisal of American National Security Policy During the Cold War*, New York: Oxford University Press, 2005, pp. 125–196.

damage, while high, would nevertheless be significantly lower than if urban-industrial areas were also attacked."[3]

In short, if the Soviet Union attacked the West with nuclear weapons, Washington should retaliate with limited nuclear strikes on Soviet military forces, announce that strategic weapons capable of annihilating urban areas were held in reserve, and negotiate an end to the crisis. The objective was to avoid the deliberate targeting of population centers in retaliation for a Soviet first strike. Counterforce, then, was a retaliatory strategy: If deterrence failed, counterforce aimed to limit the damage to the United States and its allies by destroying Soviet nuclear forces. Preemption was explicitly renounced.

But, as Lawrence Freedman and Jeffrey Michaels note, "it was difficult to explain why developing targets for a city-avoiding second strike was different from plans for a first strike."[4] The Kremlin would need to believe that the United States would *wait* until after a first Soviet strike to target Soviet nuclear forces, forgoing the option of mitigating that strike by acting preemptively. Indeed, the logic of only attacking an adversary's forces *in retaliation* when preemption was an option seemed strained. According to that logic, the scenario for nuclear use would require the Soviets to initiate a limited first strike, holding enough forces in reserve for the United States to attack in response. The Soviet Union did not appear to find the commitment to forgo preemption credible.

By late 1963, McNamara reversed himself. Rather than focusing on a counterforce retaliatory strike, he now argued that assured destruction provided the best deterrent effect. Moscow would never launch a first strike, he postulated, if Washington maintained the capability "to destroy . . . the Soviet government and military con-

---

[3] Lawrence Kaplan, Ronald Landa, and Edward Drea, *The McNamara Ascendancy, 1961–1965*, Washington, D.C.: U.S. Government Printing Office, 2006, p. 306. See also Deborah Shapley, *Promise and Power: The Life and Times of Robert McNamara*, Boston: Little, Brown and Company, 1993, pp. 135–146; William Kaufmann, *The McNamara Strategy*, New York: Harper & Row, 1964, pp. 102–134; Fred Kaplan, *The Wizards of Armageddon*, New York: Simon and Schuster, 1983, pp. 263–285; Francis J. Gavin, *Nuclear Statecraft: History and Strategy in America's Atomic Age*, Ithaca, N.Y.: Cornell University Press, 2012, pp. 30–56.

[4] Freedman and Michaels, 2019, p. 308.

trols, plus . . . 30% of their population, 50% of their industrial capacity, and 150 of their cities"—what he called unacceptable damage.[5] McNamara declared that assured destruction was U.S. policy and suggested that it would be better for stability if both sides had a secure second-strike capability.[6] McNamara was unequivocal that the United States could not disarm Soviet nuclear forces via a counterforce first strike. A significant portion of Moscow's nuclear arsenal would survive a U.S. attack, McNamara said, and would inflict unacceptable damage on the United States and its allies.[7] Therefore, the United States was prepared to authorize a preemptive nuclear strike only if there was concrete intelligence of an imminent Soviet attack or if an incoming Soviet missile was detected by the U.S. Ballistic Missile Early Warning System. But that qualifier of "only" nonetheless created requirements for counterforce capabilities—and, arguably, for planning. Although noting that this position is subject to debate, Austin Long's review of U.S. deterrence policy concludes "that preemptive-counterforce options were a major part of U.S. efforts to deter the Soviet Union for the entire Cold War."[8]

Under the Nixon administration, the United States, alarmed by Soviet nuclear modernization, developed the capabilities to hold much of the Soviet nuclear arsenal at risk. This required thousands of warheads to cover thousands of Soviet strategic forces buried in hardened silos and concealed at sea. Recognizing that the emergence of multiple independently targetable reentry vehicles (MIRVs) breathed new life into counterforce, the Nixon administration began equipping Minuteman III ICBMs with multiple warheads in June 1970. By December of that year, the U.S. Air Force was authorized to deploy

---

[5]   Kaplan, Landa, and Drea, 2006, p. 319.

[6]   Freedman and Michaels, 2019, p. 310.

[7]   Theodore Richard, "Nuclear Weapons Targeting: The Evolution of Law and U.S. Policy," *Military Law Review*, Vol. 224, No. 4, 2016.

[8]   Austin Long, *Deterrence—From Cold War to Long War: Lessons from Six Decades of RAND Research*, Santa Monica, Calif.: RAND Corporation, MG-636-OSD/AF, 2008, p. 28.

2,100 warheads on ICBMs—enough to imperil the lion's share of the Soviet nuclear stockpile.[9]

In January 1974, President Richard Nixon signed National Security Decision Memorandum (NSDM) 242, creating novel options for the employment of nuclear weapons, including several counterforce and/or counter-leadership employment options.[10] Under NSDM-242 and the resulting Nuclear Weapons Employment Policy (NUWEP) 74, counterforce options were not exclusively confined to retaliation following a Soviet first strike on the United States. This was a fundamental shift from the Kennedy administration's counterforce strategy. If deterrence failed, McNamara had wanted to limit the damage of a nuclear strike by destroying any Soviet nuclear forces that had not already been launched—even though, as already noted, he saw this as a futile mission. In contrast, the Nixon administration created several novel options for launching preemptive strikes on the Soviet nuclear arsenal—largely driven by contingencies involving a Soviet conventional attack on North Atlantic Treaty Organization (NATO) members in Europe.[11] As Long notes,

> NUWEP 74 made clear that it was expected that both [major-attack options] and [selected-attack options] could be executed from a force posture known as generated without damage (GWOD). This clearly meant a preemptive first strike, as U.S. forces would be at their maximum readiness (i.e., not a day-to-day alert posture) yet would not have sustained damage from a Soviet attack.[12]

More importantly, the United States now wielded the technology required to destroy a significant portion of the Soviet nuclear

---

[9] Kaplan, 1983, p. 364.

[10] National Security Council, "Policy for Planning the Employment of Nuclear Weapons," National Security Decision Memorandum 242, to Secretary of State; Secretary of Defense; Director, Central Intelligence Agency; and Director, Arms Control and Disarmament Agency, January 17, 1974.

[11] Seyom Brown, "The New Nuclear MADness," *Survival*, Vol. 62, No. 1, 2020.

[12] Long, 2008, p. 37.

stockpile. Armed with accurate, MIRVed ICBMs capable of penetrating hardened missile silos and underground command bunkers, the United States could now hold over 40,000 Soviet target installations at risk. NSDM-242 prioritized planning for nuclear strikes on the Soviet nuclear arsenal—ICBMs, intermediate-range ballistic missiles, nuclear weapon storage locations, airfields for nuclear-capable aircraft, and SSBN bases—and Soviet nuclear command, control, and communication (NC3) systems.[13]

The incorporation of counterforce options into major planning documents and the development of capabilities to implement them were driven by the need to maintain damage limitation options that kept pace with the growing Soviet arsenal. As Long notes,

> Even though most analysts had concluded that highly significant damage limitation was no longer possible with the nuclear balance as it was in 1970, the need for a plausible first strike still drove the United States to plan for damage-limiting counterforce.[14]

Incorporation of counterforce options was also seen as central to the credibility of U.S. extended deterrence guarantees. By the time Nixon took office, concern about Warsaw Pact conventional superiority in Europe was high. If mutually assured destruction produced nuclear stalemate, strategic weapons could not credibly deter Soviet conventional attack. To make strategic nuclear systems relevant in such a scenario, the United States needed to threaten first use against a credible target set. Hitting Soviet cities first was not deemed credible, so the Soviet strategic nuclear arsenal and associated systems were chosen. One former Department of Defense nuclear policymaker offered a different explanation of the relationship between counterforce and extended deterrence:

> What is necessary is the ability to limit damage to "tolerable" levels of casualties and destruction. This is so an American pres-

---

[13] Terry Terriff, *The Nixon Administration and the Making of U.S. Nuclear Strategy*, Ithaca, N.Y.: Cornell University Press, 1996, Ch. 6.

[14] Long, 2008, p. 37.

ident can persuade others that he would risk an attack on the U.S. homeland, or that he could face down a threat to attack that homeland, in the act of spreading America's protective mantle over Western Europe and other parts of the world.[15]

Equally important to these policy-driven justifications were bureaucratic and domestic politics. The U.S. armed services could rely on the counterforce mission as justification for maintaining a robust triad, and no U.S. administration wanted to be seen as falling behind the Soviets.

Yet these were not the only factors that led to the shift toward offensive counterforce under Nixon. Timothy P. McDonnell argues that Nixon saw counterforce capabilities through a geopolitical lens. He notes that "Nixon thought improved counterforce could provide something he once called 'diplomatic wallop.' . . . Bargaining advantages that accrued from nuclear strength, he believed, could help him advance his expansive geopolitical goals."[16] In short, there was a confluence of drivers—improved U.S. capabilities coming online, extended deterrence concerns in the context of perceived conventional inferiority vis-à-vis the Warsaw Pact, worries about the Soviet arsenal and the need to limit the damage of a Soviet strike; bureaucratic interests, domestic politics, and geopolitics—that all came together to produce the change.

Maintaining capabilities to deliver a prompt counterforce strike has been a driver of U.S nuclear and broader security policy ever since. U.S. planners determined that the top-priority targets were air defense, nuclear command centers, missile silos, and air bases (and, later, submarines). Being able to hit those targets as rapidly as possible once warning information was available became a top priority for U.S. war

---

[15] Earl C. Ravenal, "Counterforce and Alliance: The Ultimate Connection," *International Security*, Vol. 6, No. 4, Spring 1982, p. 32.

[16] Timothy P. McDonnell, *"Diplomatic Wallop": Nixon and the Return of Counterforce*, Cambridge, Mass.: Massachusetts Institute of Technology, Political Science Department Research Paper No. 2018-3, April 6, 2018, p. 42.

planners.[17] Without counterforce options, the United States would be limited to a city-busting massive retaliation in case of deterrence failure; this approach was seen as incredible, and, further, it would not limit the damage of any follow-on Soviet strike. Several prominent scholars disagreed with this logic, arguing that a state of affairs of mutually assured destruction eliminated all incentives for a first strike and that capabilities beyond those required to ensure retaliation were thus unnecessary.[18] But these arguments never gained currency within policymaking circles. As Austin Long and Brendan Rittenhouse Green have documented, the United States devoted extensive resources to intelligence for a counterforce strike throughout the Cold War and beyond.[19]

Indeed, despite the end of the Cold War, the collapse of the Soviet Union, and the dramatic reductions in strategic forces achieved through strategic arms control, the United States continues to maintain significant prompt counterforce capabilities. And although President Bill Clinton authorized a significant shift in U.S. nuclear policy in 1997 when he signed Presidential Directive Decision (PDD) 60, which abandoned a U.S. commitment to "prevail" in a nuclear conflict, U.S. strategic planning documents still point to the need to maintain counterforce options for damage limitation.[20] There is no evidence of ongoing U.S. planning for *preemptive* counterforce strikes, but the United States does not rule out the possibility of using nuclear weapons first. Regardless of U.S. plans or declared intentions, the United States' for-

---

[17] William Burr, "The 'Launch on Warning' Nuclear Strategy and Its Insider Critics," National Security Archive webpage, June 11, 2019. For example, the commander of Strategic Air Command in 1987 said, "The purpose of promptness is to remove warfighting resources from Soviet control, thereby disrupting and blunting the ongoing Soviet attack and limiting damage to the U.S. and our allies" (quoted in Charles L. Glaser, *Analyzing Strategic Nuclear Policy*, Princeton, N.J.: Princeton University Press, 1990, p. 246).

[18] For example, see Robert Jervis, *The Illogic of American Nuclear Strategy*, Ithaca, N.Y.: Cornell University Press, 1985; and Glaser, 1990, Ch 7.

[19] Austin Long and Brendan Rittenhouse Green, "Stalking the Secure Second Strike: Intelligence, Counterforce, and Nuclear Strategy," *Journal of Strategic Studies*, Vol. 38, Nos. 1–2, 2015.

[20] Richard, 2016, p. 947.

midable counterforce capabilities alone generate adversary threat perceptions about the possibility of using those capabilities for preemption. Even U.S. analysts reach similar conclusions, as a 2003 RAND
Corporation study notes: "What the planned force appears best suited
to provide beyond the needs of traditional deterrence is *a preemptive
counterforce capability against Russia and China.* Otherwise, the numbers and the operating procedures simply do not add up."[21]

President Barack Obama, who harbored an ambitious nuclear
risk-reduction agenda, also did not alter counterforce employment
policies. His administration unveiled a strategy document in 2013
that affirmed the U.S. commitment to maintaining counterforce targeting options. Equally important, it rejected minimum deterrence
and countervalue employment policies, though it never defined those
terms.[22] Ultimately, the logic of maintaining options for damage limitation if deterrence were to fail carried the day over more-ambitious
arguments for limiting the role of nuclear weapons within the Obama
administration.[23]

Although the 2018 Nuclear Posture Review (NPR) refrains from
discussing nuclear targeting policies, it reveals the continuing commitment to counterforce under President Donald Trump. For instance,
the NPR reiterates that damage limitation remains a paramount U.S.
objective. "If deterrence fails, the United States will strive to end any
conflict at the lowest level of damage possible and on the best achievable terms for the United States, allies, and partners," the executive
summary explains. "U.S. nuclear policy for decades has consistently
included this objective of limiting damage if deterrence fails."[24]

---

[21] Glenn Buchan, David M. Matonick, Calvin Shipbaugh, and Richard Mesic, *Future Roles of U.S. Nuclear Forces: Implications for U.S. Strategy,* Santa Monica, Calif.: RAND Corpora-tion, MR-1231-AF, 2003, p. 92. Emphasis in original.

[22] U.S. Department of Defense, *Report on Nuclear Employment Strategy of the United States Specified in Section 491 of 10 U.S.C.,* Washington, D.C., June 12, 2013.

[23] Fred Kaplan, *The Bomb,* New York: Simon & Schuster, 2020, p. 242.

[24] U.S. Department of Defense, *Nuclear Posture Review 2018,* Washington, D.C., February 2018, p. viii.

In short, the United States arrived at its current approach to deterrence requirements through a series of historically contingent twists and turns. In the early years of the Kennedy administration, counterforce was explicitly a retaliatory strike concept. The move away from an explicit commitment only to strike Soviet nuclear forces in retaliation resulted from policy evolution and the demands of the Cold War's global rivalry. And the capabilities for actually targeting a significant share of the Soviet arsenal did not come online until the late 1960s and early 1970s (although there was also a small window of U.S. predominance when the Soviets had yet to build up in the 1950s). Since then, the United States has maintained significant prompt counterforce capabilities. Keeping up the ability to target Russian forces for the contingency of a damage-limiting counterforce strike has an outsize impact on U.S. nuclear policy because of the numbers involved. Although the United States might not plan for preemption, its adversaries have every reason to assume that it does—or could do so in the future.

Soviet/Russian Nuclear Strategy and Force Development

From 'Survival Strategy' to 'Unacceptable Damage'

During the Cold War, Soviet officials rejected Western strategic theory (including the very concept of *deterrence*) for ideological reasons, but they did take inspiration from Western ideas and adopted some for their own use.[25] Admitting that nuclear war could pose an existential risk to the Soviet experiment would have violated party dogma; so, in the early years of the nuclear age, the Soviet Union aspired to a preemptive "survival strategy" that vastly outstripped the country's military and technical resources and was probably not even a theoretical possibility.[26]

---

[25] Yu. A. Pechatnov, "Teoriya sderzhivaniya: genezis," *Vooruzheniya i ekonomika*, No. 2, 2016.

[26] Yu. A. Pechatnov, "Analiz otechestvennykh i zarubezhnykh podkhodov k formirovaniyu kontseptsii i mekhanizma sderzhivaniya ot razvyazyvaniya voennoi agressii," *Vooruzheniya i ekonomika*, No. 3, 2010. On the Soviet Union's technical incapability for damage limitation,

Although Soviet analysts did not couch the problem in terms of "deterrence" and "strategic stability," they quickly realized that their country's nuclear strategy defied reality. Memoir literature recounts that they carried out research analogous to that done at the Pentagon under McNamara and that the Soviet studies drew conclusions that were similar to the U.S. ones.[27] Initial enthusiasm for national missile defenses evaporated as study after study showed that they would be ruinously expensive, of minimal effectiveness, and easily thwarted by simple adversary countermeasures.[28] Counterforce targeting for damage limitation did not fare much better.[29] The Soviet Union needed more-credible alternatives to the "survival strategy." Soviet officials took inspiration from an unlikely source: McNamara himself. Although McNamara and Westerners ever since have called the idea of strategic nuclear deterrence by threat of punishment "assured destruction," the Soviets latched onto another aspect of his formulation: "unacceptable damage." This concept and its derivatives remain central to Russian discussions of nuclear strategy and deterrence in the post-Soviet era.[30]

In Soviet and Russian nuclear strategy, the requirement to inflict unacceptable damage even after forces have been degraded by a first strike has been the core requirement for effective deterrence. Particularly in the past 20 years, Russian analysts have proposed many approaches to determining what damage the adversary will find unacceptable. Traditionally, however, Soviet strategists equated unaccept-

---

see Edward Geist, *Armageddon Insurance: Civil Defense in the United States and Soviet Union, 1945–1991*, Chapel Hill, N.C.: University of North Carolina Press, 2019, p. 158.

[27] John Hines, Ellis M. Mishulovich, and John F. Shulle, *Soviet Intentions 1965–1985*, Vol. 1, *An Analytical Comparison of U.S.-Soviet Assessments During the Cold War*, McLean, Va.: BDM Federal, 1995.

[28] A. A. Kokoshin, ed., *Vliyanie tekhnologicheskikh faktorov na parametry ugroz natsional'noi i mezhdunarodnoi bezopasnosti, voennykh konfliktov i strategicheskoi stabil'nosti*, Moscow, Russia: Izdatel'stvo MGU, 2017, Ch. 3.

[29] Vladimir Dvorkin and Aleksei Produkin, *Povest' o 4 TsNII MO i yadernoi sderzhivanii*, Yubileinyi, Russia: PTSM, 2009; Yu. Mozzhorin, *Tak eto bylo: Memuary Yu. A. Mozzhorina*, Moscow, Russia: ZAO Mezhdunarodnaya Programma Obrazovaniya, 2000.

[30] Apparently, this term was adopted from a Russian translation of McNamara's phrase (Kokoshin, 2017, Ch. 6).

able damage with the destruction of the few hundred largest U.S. cities. Moreover, where McNamara's "assured destruction" was a measure of sufficiency distinct from employment policy, Soviet and Russian military writings suggest that their nuclear war plans were *designed* to subject an attacker to unacceptable damage with retaliatory strikes.

Although Soviet analysts used a different approach than those in the United States to calculate how much was enough to inflict unacceptable damage, they came to similar answers. Alain C. Enthoven's methodology led to a conclusion that 400 1MT (megaton) warheads would be sufficient for "assured destruction."[31] In the Soviet Union, Andrei Sakharov suggested that 500 1MT warheads would be enough to inflict unacceptable damage on the United States.[32] In both superpowers, the estimate of nuclear forces needed for assured destruction followed a similar downward path after the 1960s. Late Soviet and post-Soviet Russian sources commonly give a figure of 150MT delivered as enough to meet the unacceptable damage requirement. They also seem to have concluded that, between a possible U.S. counterforce first strike and potential missile defenses, large arsenals were necessary to ensure a 150MT retaliation. Apparently, unacceptable damage was (and presumably is) treated as a binary threshold: Delivering 149MT is considered insufficient for deterrence.[33] Instead of trying to match U.S. capabilities quantitatively or qualitatively, the Soviet Union would field weapons sufficient to ensure that the United States would never escape unacceptable damage irrespective of its investments in counterforce weapons and missile defenses.[34]

---

[31] Alain C. Enthoven and K. Wayne Smith, *How Much Is Enough? Shaping the Defense Program, 1961–1969*, New York: Harper & Row, 1971, pp. 207–208.

[32] Dvorkin and Prokudin, 2009, p. 41.

[33] S. V. Siver, V. D. Roldugin, and N. N. Tatsyshin, "Metodicheskii podkhod k analizu boevoi ustoichivosti perspektivnoi gruppirovki RVSN v usloviyakh vliyaniya faktorov neopredelennogo kharaktera," *Strategicheskaya stabil'nost'*, No. 3, 2018, pp. 22–25. This article points out the inadequacy of this binary threshold and proposes an updated methodology to address it.

[34] A. A. Kokoshin, "Asimmetrichnyi otvet nomer odin," *Nezavisimoe voennoe obozrenie*, July 27, 2007; Kokoshin, 2017, Ch. 3.

Once the Soviets had established an early warning system in the 1970s, their focus was on using strategic forces in a "retaliatory-meeting strike," commonly translated as launch-on-warning; preemption (at the strategic level) was effectively renounced altogether. As one former Soviet General Staff senior officer recalled,

> If one looks at the realities, at the balance of relative capabilities, at the weapons that the Soviet Union had and that the United States had, you would realize that we just could not have set such a task for ourselves. Our main goal—our main concern—was to ensure our own retaliatory strike capability . . . We were afraid that the U.S. could just wipe out . . . the strategic forces that we had, and then dictate their conditions to us. . . . during all that time we just could not set ourselves the task of delivering a nuclear first strike against the United States.[35]

Indeed, even though the Soviets had thousands of weapons in their arsenal by the 1970s, Long and Green note that recent archival evidence suggests that "the Soviet Union feared American counterforce innovations were undermining its deterrent [and] threatening its long-term fitness."[36]

Interestingly, it does not appear that the Soviet Union and, later, Russia considered damage limitation strikes to be a plausible option for a preemptive strategic strike. One group of nuclear scientists stated that the Soviet Union considered three requirements in determining the quantity of weapons needed: inflicting unacceptable damage in a first strike, inflicting unacceptable damage in a retaliatory strike, and preemptive disarming strikes ("when the retaliation of the enemy is *impossible*"). There was no doubt about the Soviet Union's ability to carry out the first; there was debate about the second; but no one thought the Soviet

---

[35] "SALT II and the Growth of Mistrust: Conference #2 of the Carter-Brezhnev Project: A Conference of U.S. and Russian Policymakers and Scholars Held at Musgrove Plantation, St. Simons Island, Georgia 6–9 May 1994," transcript, excerpt of May 7, Morning Session, National Security Archive, pp. 33–35.

[36] Brendan Rittenhouse Green and Austin Long, "The MAD Who Wasn't There: Soviet Reactions to the Late Cold War Nuclear Balance," *Security Studies*, Vol. 26, No. 4, 2017, p. 639.

Union could disarm the United States or that attempting to develop capabilities to do so was plausible. The concept of a preemptive strike to minimize damage is absent completely.[37]

It should be noted, of course, that the Soviet Union did take practical steps that made damage limitation more plausible, such as increasing the accuracy of warheads, even though there was no political mandate to develop preemptive options. Yet recent archival evidence suggests that even during its ambitious buildup of the 1970s, the Soviet Union's main goal, as Pavel Podvig writes, "was to build a strategic force that could survive a nuclear strike or launch a retaliatory strike while under attack. Nothing in the documents or in the details of the individual programs suggests that a first strike against the United States was an objective."[38]

Post–Cold War Nuclear Strategy

The unraveling of the Soviet Union led to some significant changes in Russian nuclear strategy; for example, unburdened from Soviet ideology, Russian officials now fully embraced deterrence as the goal of nuclear policy.[39] However, the emphasis on ensuring unacceptable damage in retaliation remained central to Moscow's approach. And with Russia's conventional military power in precipitous decline in the 1990s, nuclear weapons seemed like the only available instrument for protecting Moscow's security interests. Russian officials also began to be more and more concerned about the longer-term viability of their nuclear retaliatory capabilities. Even with the dramatic reductions stipulated by the START Treaty, signed in 1991, Russia was in a poor position to maintain the strategic nuclear forces it had inherited from the Soviet Union.

---

[37] I. A. Andryushin, A. K. Chernyshev, Yu. A. Yudin, *Ukroshchenie yadra: Stranitsy istorii yadernogo oruzhiya i yadernoi infrastruktury SSSR*, Sarov, Russia: Tipografiya «Krasnyi Oktyabr'», 2003, p. 181.

[38] Pavel Podvig, "The Window of Vulnerability That Wasn't: Soviet Military Buildup in the 1970s—A Research Note," *International Security*, Vol. 33, No. 1, Summer 2008, p. 137.

[39] Pechatnov, 2016, p. 28.

Since Russia's economic recovery in the 2000s, the situation has stabilized somewhat. Indeed, Russia has embarked on the modernization of all three legs of its triad. What does Russian nuclear modernization tell us about Russia's deterrence requirements? There is no sign of the development of large-scale counterforce capabilities that would be needed for the Soviet preemptive "survival strategy." At the same time, modern Russian ballistic and cruise missiles are much more accurate than their Soviet predecessors and can readily destroy hardened targets, such as missile silos. Russia could plausibly conduct both counterforce and countermilitary demonstration strikes, but meaningful damage limitation lies out of reach because Russian stockpiles are too small and U.S. nuclear forces are predominantly sea-based. Indeed, although the U.S. and Russian arsenals are now ostensibly equal by New START counting rules, there are huge differences between the two countries' force structures and postures. By many measures, the U.S. arsenal is quantitatively and qualitatively superior.[40]

Russia is committed to maintaining a secure, robust, and diversified assured retaliation capability for the indefinite future. Its force is designed to retain its ability to inflict unacceptable damage.[41] Significant numbers of warheads on MIRVed systems combine with smaller numbers of "assured retaliation" weapons to hedge against political and technological uncertainty. Many Russian defense thinkers say that an arsenal of at least the current size is necessary to achieve these objectives. Neither Russian official statements nor Russia's military procurement are consistent with the pursuit of a first-strike counterforce capability, but its modern weapons have the ability to destroy hardened targets.

---

[40] Lieber and Press, 2017.

[41] N. P. Ramoshkina, "Shirokomashtabnaya PRO SShA: Na puti k sozdaniyu 'pol'notsennoi' protivoraketnoi oborony," *Strategicheskaya stabil'nost'*, No. 2, 2018.

CHAPTER THREE

Defining the Problem

As the previous chapter demonstrated, despite a shared understanding about the importance of maintaining sufficient retaliatory capability to ensure deterrence, Washington and Moscow find themselves in very different positions in terms of the requirements created by the bilateral stability paradigm.

The United States maintains significant prompt counterforce capabilities and has committed to having options for damage limitation. Its own forces are structured in such a way as to make a counterforce attack all but futile. U.S. ICBMs are now de-MIRVed, reducing use-them-or-lose-them concerns. More importantly, its submarine-launched ballistic missiles (SLBMs), which account for the majority of the United States' strategic forces, provide a guarantee of retaliatory capability. Indeed, U.S. officials have not publicly expressed concern about the prospect that post-Soviet Russia might be able to successfully target the U.S. strategic force in a counterforce strike. The United States has a variety of concerns about Russia's strategic activities, from its maintenance of a large arsenal of nonstrategic nuclear weapons to its noncompliance with arms control treaties, but, as of this writing, Washington is not preoccupied by fears of counterforce Russian strikes on its nuclear forces.

The same, however, cannot be said of Russia. Fear of counterforce preemption has been a core driver of Moscow's nuclear policies for decades. Since the 1970s, Moscow's focus has been on ensuring that it maintains the capabilities to retaliate after a U.S. first strike. With the decline in Russian capabilities after the Soviet collapse, these concerns became more acute. Additionally, military developments since the end of the Cold War have compounded the challenge Russian planners face in ensuring sufficient retaliation for effective deterrence.

In short, whereas the U.S. force has significant capacity to deliver a prompt counterforce strike and its employment policy openly discusses damage limitation, the Russian emphasis is on ensuring enough retaliation to effect unacceptable damage. This chapter explores Moscow's threat perceptions and the consequences for the stability of the U.S.-Russia dyad.

Stability and Instability from Moscow's Perspective

Often, the core of Russia's concerns is lost in the debate about specific capabilities, concepts, or arms control treaties. Many argue, for example, that Russia objects to U.S. missile defense because sites have been established in countries of the former Warsaw Pact, thus encroaching on Moscow's alleged sphere of influence.[1] However, Russian officials have long been clear that their primary concern—perhaps even preoccupation—has been ensuring retaliation following a potential first U.S. strike. The widespread belief is that the certainty of Russia's ability to inflict unacceptable damage in a retaliatory strike is all that prevents the United States from undertaking (or threatening) aggressive actions against Russia. In an oft-cited 2019 article in *Military Thought*, a group of Russian Ministry of Defense (MoD) strategists characterized the ability to threaten assured retaliation as the "foundation" of deterrence at all phases of conflict.[2]

Challenges Related to Strategic Offensive Capabilities

Moscow's belief that it must have the capability to inflict unacceptable damage in a retaliatory strike after the United States has attempted to

---

[1]   Bilyana Lilly, *Russian Foreign Policy Toward Missile Defense: Actors, Motivations, and Influence*, Washington, D.C.: Lexington Books, 2014.

[2]   A. E. Sterlin, A. A. Protasov, and S. V. Kreidin, "Sovremennye kontseptsii i silovykh instrumentov strategicheskogo sderzhivaniya," *Voennaya mysl'*, No. 8, 2019.

disarm it with a counterforce first strike compels the Russian military to maintain a large number of deployed strategic warheads. However, the requirements for what counts as *unacceptable* damage are murky, as are Russian assessments of U.S. capacity to target Russian forces. The MoD's official dictionary defines *unacceptable damage* as, "In nuclear war, the magnitude of expected losses a state would incur as a result of the retaliatory strike of its adversary, which would make impossible (disadvantageous) the unleashing or continuation of war against it."[3] But it gives no insight into how the MoD calculates what it believes would constitute unacceptable damage for the United States.[4]

The waters have been further muddied as Russian strategists have been experimenting with several related concepts. Some Russians argue that the entire concept of "unacceptable damage" is outdated and should be junked altogether. For instance, a 2012 Institute of World Economy and International Relations of the Russian Academy of Sciences (IMEMO) publication edited by Alexei Arbatov, Vladimir Dvorkin, and Sergei Oznobishchev proposed replacing "unacceptable damage" with a criterion based on the "balance of second-strike potentials."[5] MoD-affiliated strategists subsequently penned an article-length rebuttal arguing for the continued relevance of such "objective" deterrence criteria as "unacceptable damage."[6] But it is not clear how to calculate how much is enough to deter a particular adversary. Russian authors have proposed methodologies using such tools as fuzzy sets and

---

[3] Russian Ministry of Defense, "Nepriemlemyi ushcherb," webpage, undated.

[4] Some have suggested that the number of warheads required to inflict unacceptable damage significantly decreased in the post–Cold War context. See A. G. Burutin, G. N. Vinokurov, V. M. Loborev, S. F. Pertsev, and Yu. A. Podkorytov, "Kontseptsiya nepriemlemogo ushcherba: genezis, osnovnye prichiny transformatsii, sovremennoe sostoyanie," *Vooruzhenie. Politika. Konversiya*, No. 4, 2010. Concrete numbers are hard to come by, although one group of MoD-affiliated strategists has written that 100 warheads of 1MT would suffice. Cited in Michael Kofman, Anya Fink, and Jeffrey Edmonds, *Russian Strategy for Escalation Management: Evolution of Key Concepts*, Washington, D.C.: CNA, April 2020, p. 31.

[5] Alexei G. Arbatov, Vladimir Z. Dvorkin, and Sergei K. Oznobishchev, eds., *Rossiya i dilemmy yadernogo razoruzheniya*, Moscow, Russia: Institute of World Economy and International Relations of the Russian Academy of Sciences, 2012, p. 16.

[6] V. M. Burenok and Yu. A. Pechatnov, "O kriterial'nykh osnovakh yadernogo sderzhivaniya," *Vooruzheniya i ekonomika*, No. 1, 2013, p. 25.

mathematical psychology to actualize their conceptual frameworks—but, even if these approaches are sound, how can one get accurate data to feed into them?[7]

The 2010 Military Doctrine calls for the ability to inflict "specified" (*zadannyi*) damage, which various analysts have interpreted in different ways.[8] Other concepts, such as "deterrent damage," have also emerged recently.[9] Russian specialists interviewed for this report suggested that the General Staff likely maintains complex quantitative formulas for determining requirements for retaliation, but the "specified damage" concept gives more flexibility for determining how much is enough.[10] In short, although the exact number of warheads that the Russian military has specified as necessary for ensuring unacceptable damage in retaliation remains unknown, it is clear that the requirements for a retaliatory strike are significant.

Since the 1990s, Russian strategists have fretted about their country's ability to fulfill those requirements. For example, a group of nuclear experts from the nuclear research institutes in Sarov used basic mathematical models to determine the probability of success for a U.S. first strike. As of 1991, the U.S. *first-strike potential*, calculated as the number of ICBMs and SLBMs that could be delivered simultaneously, reduced by 20 percent (the assumed failure rate), divided by the targeted Soviet ICBMs, was 1.12. In other words, the U.S. first-strike force was capable of delivering just over 1 strategic warhead to each Soviet ICBM, which, these experts said, in practice ruled out a

---

[7]   Burenok and Pechatnov, 2013, p. 27.

[8]   President of Russia, Voennaya doktrina Rossiiskoi Federatsii, February 5, 2010. See commentary on specified damage in Markell Boitsov, "Terminologiya v voennoi doktrine," *Nezavisimoe voennoe obozrenie*, October 31, 2014. According to a Russian encyclopedia of disarmament terms (PIR-Tsentr, "Yadernyi ushcherb," Yadernoe nerasprostranenine: Kratkaya entsiklopediya, undated), the term refers to the level of destruction of the airborne forces, the armed forces, military and state command systems, the population, or other affected enemy resources established by the military-political leadership of the state (military command bodies, command) to achieve strategic goals and objectives in the war. Moreover, at the extreme, "specified" damage can be equated with "unacceptable" damage.

[9]   See Kofman, Fink, and Edmonds, 2020, p. 40.

[10]   Author interviews with Russian experts, Moscow, December 2019.

first strike because unacceptable retaliation was ensured. As of 1999, that number was 3.35, a threefold expansion of U.S. first-strike capabilities, which represented a "threat that Russia would lose its nuclear deterrent."[11] As one Russian strategist writes, "In the 21st century, the seriousness of the issue of preserving and maintaining the deterrent potential of the strategic nuclear forces is reaching the level of the nuclear challenge for the Soviet Union in the late 1940s."[12] Today, the Russian government's consistently stated position that it does not believe further bilateral reductions below New START levels are possible suggests that Moscow remains concerned that it might not be able to fulfill its deterrence requirements with fewer warheads. Although many would dispute the math that goes into creating these requirements, the resulting threat perceptions are genuinely held and appear to be a key driver of Russian policy.

Additional Challenges to Strategic Stability

Russia's confidence in its ability to ensure retaliation has been steadily eroding over the course of the post-Soviet period for several reasons in addition to the decline in its strategic nuclear forces relative to those of the United States. Moscow's concern that the United States could, through a combination of capabilities, eventually credibly threaten to disarm Russia has grown as the gap in relevant military technological advances has widened. It is important to emphasize that the concern stems from the consequences of a combination of these capabilities, such as conventional precision-guided missiles (CPGMs), BMDs, cyber, space, and the improvements to the U.S. nuclear triad itself. Here, we briefly describe stated Russian concerns about the first two of these capabilities as an illustration of the links that Moscow sees between those capabilities and the ability to ensure retaliation.

---

[11] Andryushin, Chernyshev, and Yudin, 2003, pp. 202–204.

[12] S. T. Brezkun, *Mech ili vesy? Yadernyi faktor v probleme voiny i mira*, Sarov, Russia: FGUP «RFYaTs-VNIIEF», 2016, pp. 531–532.

Conventional Precision-Guided Missiles

In an article on CPGMs, which he calls nonnuclear strategic weapons, current Russian Ambassador to the United States and former Deputy Minister of Defense Anatoly Antonov suggests that "they can carry out missions that are today in the exclusive purview of strategic nuclear weapons."[13] Some alarmist Russian accounts have estimated that CPGMs could fulfill up to 90 percent of the missions assigned to U.S. strategic nuclear weapons.[14] Although other Russian strategists have disputed the ability of cruise missiles to threaten the country's strategic arsenal,[15] the general consensus appears to be that CPGMs could, in the future, successfully neutralize a significant number of strategic targets. The Russian view is that the U.S. capabilities in this arena are growing both qualitatively and quantitatively.[16]

Antonov also observes that "the threshold of decision-making for using [CPGMs] may be much lower than with strategic nuclear weapons."[17] Taken together with their ability to hold strategic targets at risk, CPGMs might eventually represent a counterforce capability that could be employed without breaking the nuclear taboo. Antonov assumes that a U.S. President would be much more inclined to consider a counterforce strike as a result.

Ballistic Missile Defenses

Russian estimates of the capabilities of U.S. BMD systems are notorious for what U.S. experts consider their threat inflation—specifically

---

[13] Anatoly Anin [Antonov], "Vliyanie strategicheskikh nastupatel'nykh vooruzhenii v neyadernom osnashchenii na strategicheskuyu stabil'nost'," *Mirovaya ekonomika i mezhdunarodnye otnosheniya*, No. 6, 2011, p. 45. (Antonov wrote under the pen name "Anin.")

[14] "D. Rogozin: SShA za pervye chasy voiny mogut unichtozhit' 90% raket RF," *RBK*, June 28, 2013.

[15] D. E. Akhmerov, E. N. Akhmerov, and M. G. Valeev, "Uyazvimost' kontseptsii neyadernogo razoruzheniya strategicheskikh yadernykh sil Rossii," *Vestnik Akademii voennykh nauk*, No. 1, 2016.

[16] V. P. Krasnoslobodtsev, A. V. Raskin, S. S. Savel'ev, and O. S. Kupach, "Analiz vozmozhnosti po realizatsii SShA kontseptsii bystrogo global'nogo udara," *Strategicheskaya stabil'nost'*, No. 2, 2014.

[17] Anin [Antonov], 2011, p. 45.

about the systems' ability to threaten Russian strategic nuclear forces. In Russian thinking, U.S. BMD plays the role of an added insurance policy, mopping up any Russian missiles that were not eliminated by the first strike. According to the former head of the General Staff, Gen. Yuri Baluevsky, future U.S. missile defenses might be able to absorb any retaliatory capability Russia could muster: "Their ultimate dream is to intercept 100 missiles," he asserted, "and ensure themselves invulnerability after a first strike."[18]

Lt. Gen. Viktor Poznikhir, the first deputy director of the Main Operations Department of the General Staff, has stated that Russia estimates that the United States will field more than 1,000 BMD interceptors by 2022, and, "in the future, [they] will outnumber the quantity of Russia's deployed strategic warheads."[19] He has described modeling conducted by the General Staff that concluded that the U.S. Standard Missile 3 block 2A interceptor, currently deployed as part of the European Phased Adaptive Approach, was capable of shooting down Russian ICBMs in the boost phase.[20] Neither of these estimates would be considered credible by U.S. experts, but the Russian military might well believe them. Indeed, that would seem to be the case, given how consistently Russian officials, analysts, and strategists voice these assessments.

Regardless of Moscow's views on the capabilities of current U.S. systems, Russia's broader focus appears to be on the lack of limits on future U.S. development of antiballistic missile (ABM) systems following Washington's decision to leave the ABM treaty in 2002. According to Antonov, the key question for Moscow is "how to achieve predictability in terms of U.S. plans for BMD"[21]—a question for which he does not have an answer. Absent limits on U.S. capabilities, Russian

---

[18] Aleksandr Pronin, "Gonka za global'nym prevoskhodstvom," *Rossiiskoe Voennoe Obozrenie*, No. 4, April 2013, pp. 56–57.

[19] Viktor Poznikhir, speech given at the 8th Moscow International Security Conference, April 23, 2019.

[20] See Ekaterina Tomilenko, "Opasnym kursom," *Krasnaya zvezda*, October 11, 2016.

[21] Anatoly Anin [Antonov], "Pro Ssha—podryvayushchii doverie potentsial," *Mirovaya ekonomika i mezhdunarodnye otnosheniya*, No. 3, 2012, p. 13.

strategists engage in worst-case scenario thinking, which leads them to conclude that it is only a matter of time before the United States develops BMD capabilities that could credibly threaten to thwart Moscow's retaliatory capability. Such a development, in turn, would increase U.S. willingness to strike first. As Poznikhir said, "The U.S. global BMD system lowers the threshold for nuclear use, since it creates the 'illusion' of impunity for a strategic nuclear attack under 'the umbrella of missile defense.'"[22]

Several Russian officials have noted that the combination of CPGMs and BMDs creates a particularly alarming contingency. As Antonov writes, "CPGM in combination with the development of global BMD systems could under certain circumstances transform into a powerful military capability that creates the illusion of the ability to carry out a disarming first strike."[23] In this scenario, the United States could effectively disarm Russia without using nuclear weapons.

Summary

Although BMD and CPGMs represent perhaps the two most prominent capabilities of concern to Moscow, they are best seen as symptoms of a broader phenomenon. The contingencies described by Russian officials when these capabilities could be employed against Russia are all preemptive counterforce scenarios. Other U.S. capabilities that also cause Moscow concern in the context of the strategic relationship—such as cyber, placement of weapons in space, and the fielding of low-yield warheads—are discussed in the context of such scenarios. Cyber, for example, could be used to undermine NC3, providing a left-of-launch counterforce effect.[24] One Russian analyst writes that

> [All] cutting-edge American military technologies are intended to devalue Russia's nuclear weapons . . . Unmanned vessels and undersea drones can autonomously track SSBNs for protracted

---

[22] Poznikhir, 2019.

[23] Anin [Antonov], 2011, pp. 45–46.

[24] "V Genshtabe rasskazali o tselyakh sozdaniya amerikanskoi sistemy PRO," RIA-Novosti, April 24, 2019.

periods of time and neutralize them in case of danger. Space tracking and targeting systems will make mobile ground-based missile systems vulnerable. In a few years, laser weapons and neutral particle beams will become powerful enough to intercept ballistic and hypersonic missiles.[25]

Although some of these technologies are more science fiction than real threat, and the ones that are being developed are not intended to negate the Russian deterrent, the view that U.S. military-technological prowess could eventually be leveraged to engage in a counterforce disarming first strike (or to threaten one) is widely shared in the Russian security establishment.

Counterforce Concerns During Peacetime

A variety of specific scenarios involving possible U.S. counterforce strikes are described by Russian strategists. The so-called *bolt from the blue*, a strike on Russian forces outside the context of a crisis, is seen as highly unlikely. A U.S. preemptive strike during a crisis is considered more plausible. In such a scenario, damage limitation strikes and disarming strikes are almost impossible to distinguish. Furthermore, so-called *decapitation strikes*—attacks on NC3 and the political-military leadership—are considered just as destabilizing as counterforce strikes because the effect would be similar.[26]

But an additional contingency is also increasingly prominent in Russian writings and official statements: the peacetime use of a counterforce strike threat to achieve political objectives. If Washington is able to credibly threaten a disarming counterforce first strike, Moscow would be forced to concede without being able to fire a shot. As Antonov puts it, "The U.S., having effectively neutralized the

---

[25] Vadim Kozyulin, "Soedinennye Shtaty na puti k strategicheskoi neuyazvimosti," Russian International Affairs Council webpage, July 1, 2020.

[26] Indeed, Vladimir Putin himself has conflated disarming and decapitating strikes in public comments. See "Putin: Rossii nel'zya isklyuchat' opasnost' naneseniya obezoruzhi-vayushchego udara," *Vzglyad*, June 19, 2013.

nuclear weapons in a country, objectively would be able to impose its dictates on it."[27] The notion that Washington seeks to leverage strategic invulnerability to impose its dictates on countries that pursue a foreign policy that is not to its liking figures prominently in Russian writings. But as one analyst notes:

> Essentially, the United States is systematically moving towards re-creating the state of affairs of 1945, when it was the only country that had nuclear weapons, could impose its will on the entire world, and remained beyond the reach of the armed forces of other countries.[28]

This concern has been long-standing in the Russian security establishment. But the development of additional U.S. systems capable of threatening Russia's deterrent, combined with the maintenance of significant counterforce capability in the U.S. nuclear arsenal itself, has convinced many in Moscow that this kind of geopolitical blackmail using the threat of a disarming strike is possible at some point in the near future. Therefore, Russia's concerns about preemption are relevant not only in a crisis but also during what the United States would consider a peacetime context.

Why This Matters for the United States

The United States must consider four consequences of Russia's growing concern about its ability to retaliate after a counterforce first strike. First, Moscow has developed a suite of new capabilities to address this concern. Most prominent are the systems introduced by Vladimir Putin in his March 2018 annual speech to Parliament: the Poseidon nuclear-powered long-range autonomous underwater vehicle, the Yu-71 Avangard hypersonic glide vehicle, the RS-28 Sarmat heavy liquid-fueled ICBM, the Kinzhal air-launched aeroballistic missile, and the Bure-

---

[27] Anin [Antonov], 2011, p. 50.

[28] Kozyulin, 2020.

vestnik nuclear-powered cruise missile.[29] In an October 2019 interview, the Russian president said that these systems were developed following the U.S. withdrawal from the ABM treaty, which "was the cornerstone of the entire global strategic security system . . . [because] it made clear that neither party can ever win a nuclear war, should it happen. That was the whole point." Because the "strategic balance must be maintained," such "offensive weapons that will defeat any ABM system" became necessary.[30] Putin promised to field new weapons guaranteeing that Washington will always be threatened with "unacceptable damage." Some of these capabilities, it has been argued, add instability to the relationship and increase the prospects of unintended conflict or catastrophic accident. Regardless, it is clear that the new systems were almost exclusively developed to ensure Russia's ability to retaliate in the context of the U.S. departure from the ABM treaty and increased U.S. counterforce capabilities.[31] As of this writing, it would be an exaggeration to call this arms-race instability in the traditional, Cold War–era understanding of the term. However, Moscow's pursuit of novel nuclear weapons is certainly a national security concern for the United States.

Second, Russia seems unwilling to reduce its strategic nuclear forces below New START levels as a result of the requirements to ensure unacceptable damage in retaliation. Many Russian officials and defense intellectuals contend that Moscow needs large strategic nuclear forces as a hedge against the possibility that the United States could exploit a combination of a counterforce first-strike and related capabilities (such as BMD) to escape unacceptable damage.[32] If the United

---

[29] President of Russia, "Poslanie prezidenta federal'nomu sobraniyu," March 1, 2018. The Sarmat is a conventional ICBM like the SS-18 and SS-19 and was planned to replace them, although its silos may be protected by a close-in defense system, Mozyr'.

[30] President of Russia, "Interview with Al Arabiya, Sky News Arabia and RT Arabic," October 13, 2019.

[31] Austin Long, "Red Glare: The Origin and Implications of Russia's 'New' Nuclear Weapons," *War on the Rocks*, March 26, 2018.

[32] V. I. Kovalev, "Yadernoe oruzhie i sreda bezopasnosti Rossii v XXI veke," *Strategicheskaya stabil'nost'*, No. 3, 2014, p. 19.

States wishes to continue to reduce its reliance on nuclear weapons and engage in mutual reductions with Russia, Moscow's concerns about preemption pose a significant problem.

Third, the overall stability of the bilateral relationship, and thus its ability to deliver on U.S. national interests, has eroded, in no small part because of divergences over strategic issues. Although there are many causes of the downturn in U.S.-Russia relations (most of which do not relate to the strategic balance), Moscow's concerns about preemption and the lack of a bilateral framework to address them reinforce zero-sum thinking about the relationship and empower worst-case scenario approaches. Given the centrality of the bilateral deterrence paradigm to Russian understandings of national security, the prospect that Russian capabilities no longer effectively deter the United States—that Washington is seeking and will eventually achieve strategic invulnerability—makes cooperation on shared interests nearly impossible and removes guardrails to highly assertive Russian actions. The fear of nuclear blackmail in peacetime is compounded by the widely shared view in Russia that the United States systematically seeks to overthrow the regimes of its geopolitical rivals.

Finally, a strong case can be made that Russian concerns about preemption might incentivize a first strike in a serious crisis. The United States has an interest in ensuring that Russia is not driven to initiate a strategic exchange over use-them-or-lose-them concerns. That interest is reinforced by the reality that the U.S. ability to limit damage from a Russian strike is, in fact, quite circumscribed. A recent study suggests that it would even be difficult to do so vis-à-vis China's far smaller nuclear arsenal.[33]

---

[33] Charles L. Glaser and Steve Fetter, "Should the United States Reject MAD? Damage Limitation and U.S. Nuclear Strategy Toward China," *International Security*, Vol. 41, No. 1, Summer 2016.

CHAPTER FOUR

U.S. Policy Considerations

Seven decades after the U.S.-Soviet/Russian nuclear deterrence relationship began, it is under increasing strain. Russia's concern about its ability to ensure retaliation has grown to the point where crisis stability, arms-race stability, and the overall stability of the relationship have been put at risk. However, there are several beneficial impacts for U.S. national security associated with current U.S. nuclear policy that must be balanced against these negative consequences. This chapter succinctly describes those benefits. Any potential change to U.S. policy to address the instability described in the previous chapter should be assessed in terms of that change's effect on the benefits associated with the status quo. Ideally, those benefits should not be forfeited in making changes to it; if those benefits would be negated by proposed changes, the United States should carefully weigh the trade-offs.

Benefits of the Status Quo

Deterrent Benefits

Despite the intensity of the global confrontation of the Cold War, there was no direct clash between the superpower rivals. Indeed, a strong case can be made that nuclear deterrence, based in part on U.S. counterforce capabilities, appeared to play a significant role in deterring a superpower conflict in the latter half of the 20th century.[1] Unlike in

---

[1] For example, see John Gaddis, "The Long Peace: Elements of Stability in the Postwar International System," *International Security*, Vol. 10, No. 4, Spring 1986.

previous decades, there was no direct great power conflict in the postwar period. And there has been no conflict in the years since the end of the Cold War. There is a relative consensus among scholars and analysts that U.S. nuclear posture has proven an effective deterrent against potential Soviet/Russian aggression, although such assertions are, by definition, based on a counterfactual logic: There is no way to know whether Moscow would have behaved differently under different circumstances. U.S. extended deterrence also proved effective under the current paradigm; the Kremlin refrained from attacking U.S. treaty allies during the Cold War and the post–Cold War period. This was particularly important to nonnuclear NATO allies on the front lines of a potential Cold War–era conflict in Europe—for example, West Germany, which lacked independent nuclear arsenals to deter the Soviets. It remains important to U.S. allies today.

Yet the deterrent benefit of U.S. nuclear posture vis-à-vis both the Soviet Union and Russia has been limited. Moscow has not launched direct aggression against the United States or its allies since the advent of nuclear weapons. But short of that threshold, both the Soviet Union and Russia have been willing to undertake highly assertive steps that run contrary to U.S. interests. As Freedman and Michaels note, it is hard to identify a "'golden age of deterrence,' when the Soviet Union had been kept absolutely passive by an imposing US arsenal."[2] After the Cold War, despite post-Soviet Russia's dramatically attenuated nuclear capabilities, Moscow was not deterred from challenging Washington in theaters from Ukraine to cyberspace.

Moreover, it is not clear that maintaining the current U.S. nuclear posture is necessary to obtain even that level of deterrent benefit. It is not implausible that the Soviet Union was, and Russia is, deterred from engaging in aggression against the United States and its allies because of the threat of nuclear retaliation alone (for which counterforce capabilities are unnecessary). That said, it is also not implausible that Washington's maintenance of capabilities that exceed requirements for retaliation has deterred Moscow from certain actions. It

---

[2]   Freedman and Michaels, 2019, p. 421.

should be noted that there is no compelling evidence to prove either assertion definitively.

Damage Limitation

Although the possibility that a disarming strike against Russia could succeed is minimal, a counterforce strike could nonetheless be useful in limiting the damage of a Russian attack if deterrence fails. In the context of a crisis, if the United States becomes convinced that Moscow has launched—or is imminently preparing to launch—an attack, then the President should have the option, so the argument goes, to strike Russian forces in such a way that, as best as possible, neutralizes Moscow's ability to inflict damage on the United States. The 2018 NPR maintains that "if deterrence fails, the United States will strive to end any conflict at the lowest level of damage possible and on the best achievable terms for the United States, allies, and partners."[3] As Charles Glaser and Steve Fetter write, "The damage-limitation question arises when a country is already in a severe crisis or war and the leader believes that the adversary may launch a massive nuclear attack against her country. The choice at this point is between possibly suffering a first strike and definitely suffering a second strike."[4] Maintaining robust counterforce capabilities and related employment plans—backed up by extensive intelligence, surveillance, and reconnaissance—is required for effective damage limitation.

Hedging

Both to guarantee survivability and maintain options for damage limitation, the United States has relatively large numbers of both deployed and nondeployed strategic nuclear warheads, as well as a diverse triad of delivery vehicles. This, in turn, creates redundancies in the force and allows for "hedging against potential technical problems or vulnerabilities," as the 2010 NPR notes.[5] For instance, if Moscow disarmed U.S.

---

[3] U.S. Department of Defense, 2018, p. viii.

[4] Glaser and Fetter, 2016, p. 60.

[5] U.S. Department of Defense, *Nuclear Posture Review Report*, April 2010, p. 21. In the past, the term *hedge* had been used more narrowly to refer to the U.S. nondeployed strategic

ICBMs with a crippling cyberattack or counterforce strike, Washington could retaliate with SLBMs. The 2018 NPR elaborated on the U.S. understanding of *hedging*:

> Hedging strategies help reduce risk and avoid threats that otherwise may emerge over time, including geopolitical, technological, operational, and programmatic. . . . Given the increasing prominence of nuclear weapons in potential adversaries' defense policies and strategies, and the uncertainties of the future threat environment, U.S. nuclear capabilities and the ability to quickly modify those capabilities can be essential to mitigate or overcome risk, including the unexpected.[6]

What hedging means in practice, however, is subject to interpretation. Beyond maintenance of the triad and a large nondeployed reserve, the U.S. government has not specified in great detail what is required for effective hedging.[7]

Furthermore, although it is true that maintaining significant counterforce capabilities has been an important driver of overall U.S. nuclear force posture, and thus of the hedging strategy, these two objectives are not necessarily dependent on one another. For example, it is possible to envision a nuclear force that provides for effective hedging but does not have the same counterforce capability vis-à-vis Russia. It is also possible to maintain robust counterforce options with less capacity to hedge because the bomber leg of the triad and nondeployed reserve warheads are not necessary to target Russia's delivery vehicles.

Arms Control

By emphasizing numerical parity between U.S. and Russian nuclear stockpiles, the current U.S. nuclear posture facilitates arms control negotiations and agreements. Since 1969, talks between U.S. and

---

warhead stockpile.

[6]   U.S. Department of Defense, 2018, p. ix.

[7]   For one view on such details, see Aaron R. Miles, *Implementing the Hedge Strategy in the 2018 Nuclear Posture Review*, Livermore, Calif.: Lawrence Livermore National Laboratory Center for Global Security Research, January 17, 2019.

Soviet/Russian officials produced important agreements that imposed qualitative and quantitative limitations on strategic nuclear weapons. The latest treaty, the 2010 New START agreement, is built on the current paradigm. It limits both sides to 1,550 deployed strategic warheads on 700 delivery vehicles and permits intrusive on-site inspections.

Arms control agreements tamed the arms race, dramatically reduced the numbers of both sides' nuclear weapons, and created essential mechanisms for communication between the respective military establishments to increase stability and minimize the possibility of miscalculation.

U.S.-Soviet/Russian arms control was built on the principles of parity and mutual reductions. Were the United States to depart from the practice of maintaining significant counterforce capabilities, the required numbers of warheads and delivery vehicles would certainly be lower than those it maintains today. Further mutual reductions would therefore no longer be a function of a military imperative—the size of the Russian arsenal, so long as it could not threaten U.S. retaliatory capability, would no longer factor into the size and disposition of the U.S. nuclear force. The United States would no longer be effectively tethered to Russia in the same way that it is today.

Such a shift might open the door for dramatic mutual reductions, if Russia were willing to go along. But it would also represent a leap into the unknown: It cannot be determined whether the interagency and domestic political support for arms control would diminish if deprived of the strategic logic that it enjoys today. Future arms control would have to be built on new principles.

International Legality

Counterforce targeting is often contrasted with *countervalue targeting*; i.e., targeting population centers and economically significant assets. The U.S. government's position is that the deliberate targeting of non-military objects with nuclear weapons is contrary to the laws of war. The 2013 employment guidance states that

> all plans must also be consistent with the fundamental principles of the Law of Armed Conflict. Accordingly, plans will, for example, apply the principles of distinction and proportionality and

seek to minimize collateral damage to civilian populations and civilian objects. The United States will not intentionally target civilian populations or civilian objects.[8]

The *Department of Defense Law of War Manual* states clearly that "nuclear weapons must be directed against military objectives."[9] The current approach to deterring Russia, which emphasizes counterforce targeting, thus has the advantage of being consistent with those international legal directives. Justin Anderson has written that "including the law of war as an important part of planning processes for U.S. nuclear forces informs restrictions on contingencies and targets while also contributing to the case for fielding a robust nuclear deterrent force."[10] In other words, core principles of the law of war led the United States to focus on counterforce contingencies and thus contributed to maintaining the capabilities for that mission.

However, the law of war does not preclude targeting principles other than counterforce. First, the United States has explicitly reserved the right to target civilian populations under what is known as the *doctrine of belligerent reprisals*,[11] which allows for "retaliation in the form of conduct that would otherwise be unlawful, resorted to by one belligerent in response to violations of the law of war by another belligerent."[12] The doctrine has been used to justify the legality of U.S. strategic targeting for decades.[13] Application of the doctrine in this context would

---

[8]   U.S. Department of Defense, 2013, pp. 4–5.

[9]   Office of General Counsel, *Department of Defense Law of War Manual*, Washington, D.C.: U.S. Department of Defense, June 2015, p. 393.

[10] Justin Anderson, "Nuclear Weapons and the Laws of War (Cont.)," *Arms Control Wonk*, blog post, May 11, 2016.

[11] Charles J. Dunlap, Jr., "Taming Shiva: Applying International Law to Nuclear Operations," *Air Force Law Review*, Vol. 42, 1997, p. 163.

[12] U.S. Department of State, Written Statement of the Government of the United States of America Before the International Court of Justice, June 10, 1994, p. 31. As Richard writes, "Listing cities *per se* as the potential targets of attack would no longer be considered lawful, unless they were targeted pursuant to application of the doctrine of belligerent reprisal" (Richard, 2016, p. 974).

[13] Richard, 2016.

require the United States to be retaliating against an adversary first strike. Nonetheless, it does underscore the additional flexibility that the U.S. government has afforded itself in terms of its international legal obligations regarding the targeting of nuclear weapons.

Second, the deliberate targeting of civilians is not the only alternative to counterforce. For example, Hans Kristensen, Robert Norris, and Ivan Oelrich have proposed a counter-infrastructure alternative targeting paradigm, focused on militarily relevant sites but not Russia's strategic forces themselves. In smaller numbers or at lower alert levels, nuclear forces can be targeted at adversary forces without causing the same preemption concerns as today's posture does.[14] Similarly, Michael Mazarr has called for a "counterpower" approach, targeting adversary nonnuclear military capabilities.[15]

Summary

The five benefits of current posture—deterrence; damage limitation; hedging; arms control; and international legality—are clearly significant for U.S. national security. It is clear that this approach does provide for these benefits, but it is not clear that this approach is *required* to obtain them. None of the five is a binary value; some *degree* of each might be achieved under a different bilateral paradigm. Of the five, damage limitation is the most directly tied to maintenance of the status quo; after all, a damage limitation strike if deterrence fails is the only plausible contingency for counterforce strikes. If the United States were to take steps to limit its ability to conduct a prompt counterforce strike, the options available to a President in a crisis would be more limited than they are today. Specifically, if a Russian strike had been launched or was imminent, the U.S. capacity to mitigate the effects of that strike

---

[14] Hans M. Kristensen, Robert S. Norris, and Ivan Oelrich, *From Counterforce to Minimal Deterrence: A New Nuclear Policy on the Path Toward Eliminating Nuclear Weapons*, Washington, D.C.: Federation of American Scientists and The Natural Resources Defense Council, Occasional Paper No. 7, April 2009.

[15] Michael J. Mazarr, "Beyond Counterforce," *Comparative Strategy*, Vol. 9, No. 2, 1990.

would be lessened. The extent to which damage limitation would be circumscribed would, of course, depend on the specific policy changes undertaken.

CHAPTER FIVE

Possible Policy Changes

In this chapter, we review proposals, put forth by experts and former officials, for policy changes that could mitigate the instability in the U.S.-Russia deterrence relationship. We describe these proposals in brief; the reader should consult the sources cited for more-fulsome explications and critiques. We analyze these proposals *only* in the context of the issues under consideration in this report: (1) how they address the problems associated with Russian threat perceptions regarding preemption and thus improve strategic stability and (2) the extent to which they would maintain the benefits associated with the status quo described in the previous chapter. Although some of the proposals call for unilateral steps by the United States, others would require Washington to negotiate bilaterally with Moscow. We grouped these disparate approaches into the following categories: paradigm shifts in U.S. nuclear policy; structural transformations (i.e., significant changes to nuclear capabilities); and self-restraint measures. A *paradigm shift* would entail addressing preemption concerns directly by fundamentally changing U.S. nuclear policy to move away from counterforce. *Structural transformations* in the U.S. and Russian arsenals could rule out or significantly complicate prompt counterforce strikes by modifying capabilities. *Self-restraint measures* are more-modest steps that reduce preemption concerns but do not require dramatic changes in policies or capabilities.

Paradigm Shifts in U.S. Nuclear Policy

To eliminate the destabilizing effect of Russian concerns about counterforce preemption completely, the United States would have to transform its declaratory policy (the stated circumstances under which the United States would consider employment), posture, and capabilities so that they focus mainly on retaliation contingencies. In terms of declaratory policy, the most prominent proposal is no first use (NFU). NFU would represent a significant departure from current declaratory policy as stated in the 2018 and 2010 NPRs.[1] Changes that move deployment and employment policies away from maintenance of counterforce capabilities have been referred to using the term *minimum deterrence*. Although proposals under this rubric vary in their details, they shift U.S. nuclear policy to focus on ensuring retaliation rather than on maintaining capabilities that could be used for counterforce preemption. These proposals focus on changes in numbers, posture, and/or targeting to essentially implement a declaratory policy of NFU. They can therefore be viewed as two sides of the same coin.

No First Use

NFU entails pledging to use nuclear weapons only in response to a nuclear attack by another state on the United States or its allies. Like all declaratory policies, NFU is not subject to verification or compliance mechanisms.[2] Scott Sagan describes a proposed NFU pledge thusly:

> the role of US nuclear weapons is to deter nuclear weapons use by other nuclear-weapons states against the United States, our allies, and our armed forces, and to be able to respond, with an appropriate range of nuclear retaliation options, if necessary, in the event that deterrence fails.[3]

---

[1]   U.S. Department of Defense, 2018; U.S. Department of Defense, 2010.

[2]   Ankit Panda, "'No First Use' and Nuclear Weapons," Council on Foreign Relations webpage, backgrounder, July 17, 2018.

[3]   Scott D. Sagan, "The Case for No First Use," *Survival*, Vol. 51, No. 3, 2009, p. 164.

Such a declaratory policy rules out preemption options, reserving nuclear use exclusively for retaliating.

An NFU pledge, if it is credible, could thus reduce Russian fears of a counterforce strike. After all, preemption could only come as a "first use." However, the credibility of NFU pledges is often called into question by analysts. Indeed, it would be a challenge to convince Moscow that a U.S. NFU pledge was credible if it were not accompanied by changes in posture, force structure, and targeting to reflect that pledge. Senior Russian officials have repeatedly stated that they base their judgment of the threat from the United States on capabilities, not intentions. Some proponents of NFU provide ideas for what changes would be required to bring operations and posture in conformity with the proposal; others focus exclusively on declaratory policy. For the purposes of this analysis, we merely note that declaratory policy alone would probably not have a major impact on the U.S.-Russia dyad. Therefore, NFU would necessarily need to be tied to a minimum deterrence posture.

Minimum Deterrence

Minimum deterrence entails reducing the number of nuclear weapons currently deployed to a much smaller number that proponents say would still be sufficient to deter potential adversaries by the threat of retaliation. It is essentially the force posture one would expect the United States to implement if it were to adopt an NFU declaratory policy. In general, advocates of minimum deterrence claim that any adversary that can be deterred "*will* be deterred by the prospect of a counterattack, even if it consists of only a few nuclear weapons. Beyond that minimum threshold, nuclear weapons provide little additional deterrent benefit."[4] As an inherently broad concept, minimum deterrence encompasses numerous specific proposals. They vary on the proposed numbers, types, and capabilities of the nuclear systems required to deter adversary aggression. They all, however, essentially limit the role of U.S. weapons to retaliatory scenarios.

---

[4]   Jeffrey Lewis, "Minimum Deterrence," *Bulletin of the Atomic Scientists*, Vol. 64, No. 3, July/August 2008, p. 38 (emphasis in original).

For example, Bruce Blair, Jessica Sleigh, and Emma Claire Foley have put forward a detailed proposal for what they call a "deterrence-only" paradigm, which is essentially a form of minimum deterrence. At its core, the proposal would eliminate the potential for counterforce strikes by removing adversary nuclear forces as targets and instead basing deterrence "on threatening to destroy the key elements of state control and economic power" as a response to a nuclear attack.[5] Such state control and economic targets include "leadership facilities; banking, communications, and transportation networks; oil pipeline and shipping infrastructure used in petroleum exporting; electric power plants; and oil refineries and metal works plants."[6] Most importantly, these posture changes would reduce the "operational inclination toward preemption and launch on warning."[7] The proposal calls for a force restructuring to a submarine-based monad that would be supported by investments in conventional and cyber capabilities and made in conjunction with bilateral reductions negotiated with Russia. "As long as they are backed by a resilient C3 network," the authors contend, "a maximum of four to seven survivable U.S. SSBNs at sea" would dampen adversaries' inclination to use nuclear weapons in a crisis and shift U.S. policy "from first use and launch on warning to purely second-strike responses."[8]

Assessment

Clearly, a paradigm shift involving an NFU pledge and a minimum deterrence posture would address the instability in the U.S.-Russia dyad caused by the possibility of preemption. Here, we assess whether such a paradigm shift would deliver the previously discussed five benefits of current policy.

Proponents of such a shift argue that it would enhance U.S. deterrence credibility by signaling to a potential adversary that U.S. nuclear

---

[5] Bruce G. Blair, with Jessica Sleigh and Emma Clare Foley, *The End of Nuclear Warfighting: Moving to a Deterrence-Only Posture: An Alternative U.S. Nuclear Posture Review*, Princeton, N.J.: Program on Science and Global Security, Princeton University, 2018, p. 54.

[6] Blair, Sleigh, and Foley, 2018, p. 53.

[7] Blair, Sleigh, and Foley, 2018, p. 56.

[8] Blair, Sleigh, and Foley, 2018, p. 73.

weapons existed for retaliation only. If an adversary escalated a conflict to nuclear use, it would be certain that the United States would use nuclear weapons in response. Critics question whether U.S. conventional superiority and the fear of nuclear escalation "will provide the deterrent effect necessary to prevent future conventional, chemical or biological attacks."[9] More concretely, Bruno Tetrais argues that reserving nuclear use solely for retaliation "would signal those adversaries who would take such a commitment seriously that they could do *anything* to the United States or its allies without *ever* facing the risk of a nuclear response."[10] Other critics argue that an NFU policy would undermine U.S. extended deterrence commitments and could lead those states to proliferate. According to John Harvey, U.S. allies "see no-first-use as a weakening, symbolic or otherwise, of U.S. extended deterrence." In response, they could either develop nuclear capabilities themselves or "seek accommodation with regional adversaries in ways that run counter to U.S. interests."[11] Critics of minimum deterrence argue that claims of

> deterrence functioning reliably and predictably at dramatically-reduced nuclear force levels are insupportable. The historical record also suggests that nuclear weapons may, on important occasions, contribute uniquely to deterrence.[12]

These arguments are essentially impossible to resolve definitively using empirical evidence because there is no way to know how Russia (or other potential adversaries) would act in a context that has yet to materialize. That said, the argument that such a paradigm shift weakens deterrence rests on the proposition that the threat of retaliation alone is not enough to deter Russian aggression. As already noted, this

---

[9]   Keith B. Payne, "Strategic Hubris," in "Forum: The Case for No First Use: An Exchange," *Survival*, Vol. 51, No. 5, October–November 2009, p. 29.

[10]   Bruno Tetrais, "The Trouble with No First Use," in "Forum: The Case for No First Use: An Exchange," *Survival*, Vol. 51, No. 5, October–November 2009, p. 24.

[11]   John R. Harvey, "Assessing the Risks of a Nuclear 'No First Use' Policy," *War on the Rocks*, July 5, 2019.

[12]   Keith B. Payne and James Schlesinger, "Minimum Deterrence: Examining the Evidence," *Comparative Strategy*, Vol. 33, No. 1, February 2014, p. 2.

point is debatable. However, it is clear that an NFU policy would at least raise questions about the viability of deterrence.

An NFU pledge combined with a minimum deterrence posture would certainly limit the extent to which the United States could carry out damage limitation strikes, assuming the pledge was faithfully implemented in a crisis. Effective damage limitation requires maintaining capabilities that far exceed those required for retaliation. However, the circumstances under which Washington would contemplate such a strike—a Russian attack, or near certainty of an imminent attack—would likely lead decisionmakers to scrap the NFU pledge and target its (fewer) weapons at Russian forces. But the far smaller number of U.S. weapons available for a counterforce strike would minimize the effectiveness of damage limitation even if the pledge were scrapped in a crisis.

The ability of the United States to hedge against future technological changes would be limited by a minimum deterrence posture, although the extent to which that is true would depend on the specifics of that posture. Keith Payne and James Schlesinger argue that adopting a policy of minimum deterrence would lead to permanent changes in force structure that would "make recovery and adjustment very difficult, lengthy and costly in the event of a future that is darker than anticipated."[13] Some of the more-radical minimum deterrence proposals, such as moving to a monad, would essentially abandon the cross-leg hedging that current policy allows. Less radical proposals do not call for elimination of any of the legs of the triad, or even necessarily of the nondeployed reserve. So, it is possible that some degree of hedging could be maintained even under a paradigm shift.

The impact of a paradigm shift on arms control is unclear. Most proponents of NFU or minimum deterrence make the case that the United States should adopt those policies regardless of whether Russia reciprocates. If implemented unilaterally, this paradigm shift could, as noted, undermine the strategic rationale of bilateral arms control. Moreover, it is difficult to see how the United States and Russia could negotiate a bilateral move to NFU or minimum deterrence; such a

---

[13] Payne and Schlesinger, 2014, p. 76.

step reflects a unilateral reconsideration of deterrence requirements. It is possible that Russia might reciprocate if the United States were to adopt this paradigm shift unilaterally, but this seems an unlikely outcome. And if Russia were to do so, the stability provided by the verification, notification, and inspection regimes associated with arms control would then need to be tied to something other than numerical ceilings.

Finally, in terms of international law, there is a strong case that NFU is more consistent with the laws of war than current declaratory policy. Because the United States need not adopt a policy of deliberately targeting noncombatants, a minimum deterrent posture need not pose international legal challenges.

Thus, on one hand, a paradigm shift in U.S. nuclear policy—an NFU declaratory policy and a minimum deterrence posture—would significantly mitigate the instability created by counterforce preemption concerns. On the other hand, skeptics label such a shift as a starry-eyed fantasy that would imperil U.S. and allied security by weakening deterrence. Unless negotiated with Russia in return for significant concessions, it seems unlikely to be politically viable in the United States and could call into question the need for arms control, a stabilizing force in the relationship.

Structural Transformations

Mutual Partial De-Alerting

De-alerting a portion of the two sides' strategic nuclear forces—that is, taking steps to increase time-to-launch—is one possible structural transformation that would reduce concerns about prompt counterforce strikes (as well as about the prospect of inadvertent war). Although some have proposed de-alerting the entire force,[14] such a step seems far less technically, politically, and strategically viable than partial de-

---

[14] Bruce G. Blair, "De-Alerting Strategic Nuclear Forces," in Harold A. Feiveson, ed., *The Nuclear Turning Point: A Blueprint for Deep Cuts and De-Alerting of Nuclear Weapons*, Washington, D.C.: Brookings Institution, 1999.

alerting. Moreover, partial de-alerting would address preemption concerns, the focus of this report, while still allowing for possibly hundreds of nuclear weapons to remain on alert. Given our focus on the U.S.-Russia dyad, we focus here on bilateral mutual agreements to de-alert a portion of the force rather than on unilateral U.S. steps.

With fewer nuclear weapons available for a short-notice attack, a prompt counterforce strike would be effectively impossible to undertake. Strategic forces would remain survivable but would require additional days or even weeks to re-alert. Equally significant, Washington and Moscow would have new opportunities for signaling in a crisis, when they could demonstrate resolve by placing weapons on high alert or de-escalate by taking them off alert.

Partial de-alerting proposals vary in their details. For example, David E. Mosher and his colleagues describe an option of reducing the day-to-day launch readiness of 150 ICBMs on both sides.[15] Focusing exclusively on ICBMs offers the prospect of a verifiable agreement; verifying alert status of SLBMs would be much more complicated. Sergei Rogov and his coauthors proposed a more flexible approach that allows the sides to determine which weapons to de-alert. Specifically, they argue that the United States and Russia should agree to set a cap of 500 warheads from all three legs of the triad that are ready for launch within ten minutes. Both countries could maintain another 500–1,000 warheads that could be used within a few days and another 1,000 warheads at a "zero" level of readiness requiring weeks or months to be used. At these levels, both sides would be unable to launch disarming strikes against the other side while still maintaining an effective retaliatory capability. In addition, both sides could maintain the capability to build back their nuclear forces with sufficient speed if, for example, China were to attempt to achieve parity with them.[16] This proposal poses difficult verification challenges.

---

[15] David E. Mosher, Lowell H. Schwartz, David R. Howell, and Lynn E. Davis, *Beyond the Nuclear Shadow: A Phased Approach for Improving Nuclear Safety and U.S-Russian Relations*, Santa Monica, Calif.: RAND Corporation, MR-1666-NSRD, 2003.

[16] For example, see S. Rogov, V. Esin, and P. Zolotarev, "Eksperty predlagayut kompleks mer doveriya po strategicheskim vooruzheniyam," *Nezavisimoe voennoe obozrenie*, July 2, 2004; S. Rogov, P. Zolotarev, V. Kuznetsov, and V. Esin, "Strategicheskaya stabil'nost' i

Skeptics are dubious that de-alerting nuclear forces will ameliorate Russian fears of preemption. For instance, some argue that if Washington de-alerted some or all of its ICBMs, Moscow would still remain anxious about the first-strike capabilities of U.S. SLBMs (the de-alerting of which is nearly impossible to verify), precision-strike conventional forces, and BMDs, all of which could undermine Russian second-strike capabilities. Indeed, given that, as of May 2021, more than 70 percent of U.S. strategic warheads are on SLBMs,[17] partially de-alerting U.S. ICBMs might have only limited impact on Russian preemption concerns. And regardless of whether weapons are on high alert in peacetime, use-them-or-lose-them concerns would still arise in a drawn-out crisis.

In terms of the five criteria we have outlined, some have argued that de-alerting the ICBM force could be problematic for deterrence. Rebecca Hersman, William Caplan, and Bert Thompson have written that de-alerting ICBMs would reduce "the number of warheads required to eliminate the U.S. ICBM force" and would allow a potential adversary to retarget more of its arsenal toward bomber bases and SSBNs, potentially increasing the chance for an adversary's first strike. Such a step could "[undermine] the deterrent value" of U.S. nuclear weapons, potentially provoking more aggression toward the United States and its allies.[18] That said, if the partial de-alerting were mutual, such problems would be less likely to arise.

Partial de-alerting (assuming it applied only to ICBMs) would not significantly inhibit damage limitation, given the remaining number of U.S. SLBMs on high alert status. The impact of partial de-alerting on

---

yadernoe razoruzhenie v XXI veke," *Nezavisimoe voennoe obozrenie*, November 16, 2012; and S. Rogov, V. Yesin, and P. Zolotaryov, "O kachestvennoi transformatsii rossiisko-amerikanskikh otnoshenii v strategicheskoi oblasti," *Rossiiskii sovet po mezhdunarodnym delam (RSMD) Rabochaya tetrad'*, No. 7, 2013.

[17] Johnny Wolfe, "Statement of Vice Admiral Johnny Wolf, USN, Director, Strategic Systems Programs, on FY 2022 Budget Request for Nuclear Forces and Atomic Energy Defense Activities," before the Subcommittee on Strategic Forces of the Senate Armed Services Committee, Washington, D.C., May 12, 2021, p. 2.

[18] Rebecca Hersman, William Caplan, and Bert Thompson, "Bad Idea: De-Alert U.S. ICBMs," *Defense360*, December 14, 2017.

the hedging strategy, if viewed in broad terms, would be significant: It would reduce the redundancy in the force and put more onus on two of the three triad legs in a crisis. If conducted mutually, partial de-alerting would, in itself, constitute an important arms control agreement. U.S. nuclear policy's international legality would likely be unaffected.

De-MIRVing

In the 1970s, U.S. and Soviet officials began equipping long-range nuclear missiles with MIRVs, a decision with lasting ramifications in the 21st century. "MIRVs," scholars Michael Krepon and Travis Wheeler write, "propelled vertical proliferation more than any other technological advance during the first nuclear age."[19] In the Cold War, the Nixon administration and its successors pursued MIRVs in part because they were keen to enhance U.S. counterforce capabilities by creating the means to hold the entire Soviet nuclear arsenal at risk. If deterrence failed, they could limit the damage of a nuclear strike by destroying Soviet forces. But MIRVed missiles, particularly silo-based ICBMs, are a tempting target for counterforce preemption, and thus they increase use-them-or-lose-them pressures.

By de-MIRVing missiles, U.S. and Russian policymakers thus might stabilize the strategic nuclear dyad and reduce fears of preemption.[20] However, de-MIRVing does not seem to be a viable way forward. The United States has already de-MIRVed its ICBM force; only U.S. SLBMs remain MIRVed, and MIRVed SLBMs pose less of a use-them-or-lose-them concern because of the difficulty of targeting SSBNs. So de-MIRVing would only be truly relevant for Russia. However, Russia has just brought online a new generation of MIRVed ICBMs, the Sarmat. One Sarmat missile contains up to ten warheads. Russian officials argue that MIRV technology is essential to overwhelm U.S. BMD, which, they claim, could nullify their second-strike

---

[19] Michael Krepon and Travis Wheeler, "Introduction," *The Lure and Pitfalls of MIRVs: From the First to the Second Nuclear Age*, Washington, D.C.: Stimson Center, 2016, p. 13.

[20] Alexei G. Arbatov and Vladimir Dvorkin, "The Impact of MIRVs and Counterforce Targeting on the U.S.-Russian Strategic Relationship," in Michael Krepon, Travis Wheeler, and Shane Mason, eds., *The Lure and Pitfalls of MIRVs: From the First to the Second Nuclear Age*, Washington, D.C.: Stimson Center, 2016.

capabilities.[21] Putting aside concerns about BMD, Russia would be at a significant warhead disadvantage if it de-MIRVed the Sarmat. Therefore, de-MIRVing, although perhaps desirable in the abstract, seems impractical barring (a highly unlikely) Russian willingness to take unilateral steps.

Assessment

Given the lack of means to verify de-alerting of SLBMs, partial mutual de-alerting would be confined to the two sides' ICBM forces. In light of the concentration of U.S. strategic warheads on SLBMs, the impact that such a step might have on preemption concerns would be modest at best. By the same token, it would have limited effect on the five benefits associated with the status quo. Given the lack of MIRVed ICBMs in the U.S. arsenal, on the one hand, and the concentration of Russian warheads on newly fielded MIRVed ICBMs, on the other, de-MIRVing does not seem like a practical way forward to reduce preemption concerns.

Self-Restraint Measures

Ultimately, a paradigm shift would be required to eliminate the destabilizing effect of counterforce contingencies *completely*. So long as the United States maintains significant prompt counterforce capabilities and keeps open options for damage limitation strikes, Moscow will consider its capacity for effective retaliation to be at risk. However, there are measures that the United States and Russia could take either together or unilaterally that would reduce concerns about preemption without radically changing U.S. nuclear policy. These measures would provide a degree of reassurance about the parties' lack of intention to execute a preemptive counterforce strike by complicating the ability to carry out such a strike on short notice.

---

[21] Authors' interviews with Russian experts, Moscow, November 2019.

SSBN Transparency

The U.S. SSBN fleet consists of 14 *Ohio*-class submarines, of which up to 12 are operational at any one time. Each SSBN is equipped with a maximum of 20 Trident II D5 missiles.[22] As of May 2021, the SSBN fleet accounted for more than 70 percent of all deployed strategic warheads (using New START counting rules).[23] *Ohio*-class submarines undergo regular maintenance of different lengths at various intervals in their life span, as will their *Columbia*-class successors.[24]

The Russian SSBN fleet is smaller than its U.S. counterpart, consisting of ten SSBNs, of which several are likely out of service at any given time. They can carry up to 160 launchers and a maximum of 720 warheads. However, it is likely that the number of deployed warheads at any given time is closer to 600.[25] Unlike U.S. SSBNs, which can patrol in the open oceans, Russian deterrent patrols are largely confined to "strategic bastions" relatively close to Russian shores, where the subs are protected by other naval vessels.

Washington sees SSBNs as the most survivable leg of the triad, and thus the most important for ensuring a second strike. But for Russian planners, the U.S. SSBN fleet is perhaps the most plausible U.S. first-strike weapon, given both the difficulty in detecting and targeting SSBNs and their ability to get close to Russian shores. SLBMs launched near Russia would have a short time of flight and thus might not be detected in time for Moscow to ensure retaliation. For the United States, the Russian SSBN fleet is comparably less of a first-strike threat, given their confinement to bastions.

---

[22] Hans M. Kristensen and Matt Korda, "United States Nuclear Forces, 2020," *Bulletin of the Atomic Scientists*, Vol. 76, No. 1, 2020b.

[23] See Wolfe, 2021, p. 2. The U.S. Department of State regularly publishes both the aggregate number of deployed U.S. strategic warheads and the numbers of deployed SLBMs, ICBMs, and heavy bombers. As of September 1, 2020, there were 1,497 deployed warheads, and 230 SLBMs, 397 ICBMs, and 48 heavy bombers. See U.S. Department of State, "New START Treaty Aggregate Numbers of Strategic Offensive Arms," fact sheet, December 1, 2020

[24] Office of Inspector General, *Evaluation of Nuclear Ballistic Missile Submarine (SSBN) Sustainment*, Washington, D.C.: U.S. Department of Defense, June 15, 2018.

[25] Hans M. Kristensen and Matt Korda, "Russian Nuclear Forces, 2020," *Bulletin of the Atomic Scientists*, Vol. 76, No. 2, 2020a.

Despite this asymmetry, greater mutual transparency about the number of SSBNs in operation at a given time could be useful for both sides. This could be accomplished through a regular exchange of planned maintenance schedules for SSBNs over a fixed future period. Knowing that a certain number of U.S. SSBNs are undergoing maintenance at a given time would allow Russian planners not to have to account for the SLBMs on those submarines. Exchanging maintenance schedules could also help avoid misinterpretation of SSBNs' returning to patrol after a scheduled maintenance as a deliberate increase in operational missiles. This measure would provide more predictability about the actual number of operational SLBMs deployed, thus removing some uncertainty about the size of a possible U.S. counterforce strike—or rather, providing some more certainty about the smaller size of such a strike—launched from SSBNs at any given time.[26]

Another possible self-restraint measure would be a voluntary commitment not to conduct SSBN operations within a fixed distance of the Russian coast. Such a measure would ensure a minimum time of flight for SLBM launches and thus provide assurance regarding warning time. Russia could reciprocate by committing not to operate its SSBNs outside their bastions, although the value of such a commitment to the United States would be more limited unless the new *Borei*-class Russian SSBNs begin to patrol beyond the bastions.[27] To allow for verification, both sides could be given an agreed annual number of "challenges" that would call for the other side to bring all deployed SSBNs to the surface and keep them there for a short, predetermined amount of time—long enough for satellites to verify the SSBN locations but less than the time of flight of an ICBM, thus guarding against use of the procedure to target the SSBNs themselves for a preemptive strike.[28] Alternatively, such a challenge could require releasing a special beacon buoy that uniquely identifies the specific SSBN but does

---

[26] The authors are grateful to Linton Brooks for this idea.

[27] Mosher et al., 2003, p. 69.

[28] The authors are grateful to Linton Brooks for this idea.

not begin transmission for 12 hours after release, giving the submarine enough time to relocate.[29]

Commitments Regarding Future Capabilities

Additionally, both sides could commit not to undertake certain steps that would increase concerns about preemption. Banning steps that neither side has taken or even expressed an interest in taking (indeed, in some cases, one or both sides have disavowed plans ever to take), might seem counterintuitive. But these steps could provide modest stability gains.

- *Ban on depressed trajectory flight tests of SLBMs:* Such depressed trajectory launches would significantly cut time of flight and exacerbate preemption fears.[30] They have yet to be conducted, and neither side appears to have plans to do so.
- *Ban on deployment of space-to-Earth weapons:* The United States and Russia have been engaged in a diplomatic dispute over the appropriate form and content of norms governing the possible militarization of space. However, neither side appears to have plans to deploy the weapons that might be the most destabilizing: those that could strike earthbound targets from space. Some Russian analysts have argued that striking strategic forces from space would give a decisive advantage to an attacker, facilitating a coordinated disarming attack.[31] Both sides could commit not to deploy such space-to-Earth weapons despite their differences on other space weapons, such as antisatellite weapons.
- *Ban or limit on ground-based and/or air-based deployments of prompt conventional strike options in proximity to borders:* The Intermediate-Range Nuclear Forces (INF) treaty ceased to function in 2019, and there are no limits on U.S. or Russian ground-based deployments of

---

[29] Mosher et al., 2003, p. 70.

[30] Lisbeth Gronlund and David C. Wright, "Depressed Trajectory SLBMs: A Technical Evaluation and Arms Control Possibilities," *Science & Global Security*, Vol. 3, Nos. 1–2, 1992.

[31] Pavel Podvig, "Russia and Military Uses of Space," in Pavel Podvig and Hui Zhang, eds., *Russian and Chinese Responses to U.S. Military Plans in Space*, Cambridge, Mass.: American Academy of Arts and Sciences, 2008.

intermediate- and medium-range cruise or ballistic missiles. These missiles were originally eliminated in part because of the decapitation threat to Moscow. The United States has yet to announce plans for deployments of INF-range cruise or ballistic missiles to Europe. Russia has proposed a moratorium on such deployments. Washington and Moscow could negotiate a ban or self-declared limits on said deployments to limit both decapitation concerns for Russia and nuclear decoupling concerns for NATO.

Commitments Regarding Activities Related to Preemption

Additional mutual commitments could be undertaken that mitigate concerns about preemption. These commitments relate to military activities that raise such concerns.

- *Commitment not to strike NC3 and early-warning assets in a conventional conflict:* In the case of a conventional conflict involving the United States and Russia, escalation to nuclear use could be accelerated by conventional missile strikes on NC3 and early-warning assets. The sides could commit not to strike these assets in the context of a conventional war. The impact of such a pledge would be limited, given that a war would already be underway, but it might mitigate some use-them-or-lose-them concerns without sacrificing any operational requirements.
- *Commitment not to operate attack submarines near Russian SSBN bastions or U.S. coasts:* The United States could commit to keep U.S. attack submarines a certain distance away from Russian SSBN bastions in the Barents Sea and the Sea of Okhotsk. Such a step could reduce Russian concerns about the survivability of its nuclear forces, since those attack submarines would presumably target Russian SSBNs in a conflict. In return, Russia could commit to keep its attack submarines away from the U.S. coasts, where U.S. SSBNs are more easily tracked.[32]
- *Commitment to provide advance notification of increased bomber alert status:* Although bombers do not pose the same promptness

---

[32] Mosher et al., 2003.

concerns as the other legs of the triad, putting them on alert could be misinterpreted as a preparation for a preemptive strike. Both sides could agree not to do this except during training exercises and could commit to notify each other about those exercises well in advance.

Commitments Regarding Ballistic Missile Defense

Following the demise of the ABM treaty, the unconstrained development of U.S. BMD capabilities has been one of the main drivers of Russian preemption concerns. Although treaty-based limits on BMD are likely to remain politically impossible for the United States, U.S. policymakers could consider self-restraint commitments on BMD deployment plans as a way to reduce Moscow's concerns about preemption. For example, the United States could provide Russia with annual accounts of its inventory of BMD interceptors, launchers, and associated radars; its ten-year plan for any increases in that inventory; and a commitment to advance notification of any change in those plans.[33] This would amount to a politically binding, but adjustable and voluntary, numerical ceiling on missile defenses. Such a commitment could be mutual; even though Russia's BMD capabilities are more limited than those of the United States, its new air defense systems, such as the S-500, have some missile defense capability.

Assessment

Table 5.1 provides a summary of the possible self-restraint measures that could mitigate preemption fears. These measures are modest, but if several of them are implemented simultaneously, they could address the negative consequences of current policy without any dramatic changes in force structure, posture, or even employment policy. The United States would maintain all of the five benefits associated with current policy, although damage limitation strikes could be less effective because prompt counterforce strikes would become more compli-

---

[33] Steven Pifer, *Missile Defense in Europe: Cooperation or Contention?* Washington, D.C.: Brookings Institution Arms Control Series Paper #8, May 2012, p. 22.

Table 5.1
Self-Restraint Measures

Measure	Description
Increased transparency of SSBNs through exchange of maintenance schedules	Regular exchange of maintenance schedules to provide more predictability about the actual number of operational SLBMs deployed and reduce uncertainty about the size of a possible counterforce strike
Commitments not to operate SSBNs in certain areas	U.S. commitment not to conduct SSBN operations near the Russian coast to ensure a minimum time of flight for SLBM launches and thus provide assurance regarding warning time; Russian commitment not to operate SSBNs outside their bastions
Ban on depressed trajectory flight tests of SLBMs	Mutual agreement to ban depressed trajectory launches—as neither side has conducted them or indicated an intention to do so—to mitigate preemption fears
Ban on deployment of space-to-Earth weapons	Specific commitment not to deploy weapons that could strike earthbound targets from space—separately from those weapons, such as antisatellite weapons, that are currently the subject of a broader debate between the United States and Russia (and other countries) over the militarization of space
Ban or limit on ground-based and/or air-based deployments of prompt conventional strike options in proximity to borders	Bilaterally negotiated ban or unilaterally declared limits on ground-based deployments of intermediate- and medium-range cruise or ballistic missiles to limit both decapitation concerns for Russia and nuclear decoupling concerns for NATO
Commitment not to strike NC3 and early-warning assets in a conventional conflict	Commitment not to strike NC3 and early-warning assets in the context of a conventional conflict to attempt to mitigate some use-them-or-lose-them concerns without sacrificing any operational requirements
Commitment not to operate attack submarines near Russian SSBN bastions or U.S. coasts	Limitation on how close U.S. and Russian attack submarines can operate near SSBN bases to reduce concerns about survivability
Commitment to provide advance notification of increased bomber alert status	Commitment not to put bombers on alert except during training exercises and to notify the other side of those exercises well in advance
Self-restraint commitments on BMDs	Adjustable and voluntary commitment to provide the other side with annual accounts of BMD interceptors, launchers, and associated radars and a ten-year plan for any increases in that inventory, along with a commitment to provide advance notification of any change in those plans

cated to execute. The stabilizing benefits of these steps should be balanced against that consequence.

Dialogue on Preemption Concerns

U.S. policymakers could take the initiative by proposing a bilateral dialogue that systematically examines the issues that raise Russian concerns about preemption. In the past, this topic has never been addressed directly in bilateral dialogues. During the course of arms control negotiations, concerns about preemption manifest themselves indirectly—for example, in Russia's insistence on addressing U.S. BMD in the context of New START. (In the end, Moscow merely managed to preserve language about the link between offensive and defensive arms in the preamble.) The proposed dialogue would seek to bring these issues out into the open and put them directly on the table. It would be a difficult discussion, given the sensitivity of the issues at stake. But such a dialogue might be necessary to develop possible policy options that would be tailored to the specific concerns.

Such a dialogue could also examine both sides' perceived requirements for deterrence. Specifically, it would be useful to develop a shared, even if informal, understanding on minimum requirements for the "unacceptability" of a retaliatory strike. Public statements of the Russian political-military leadership seem to indicate that Moscow thinks such a second strike needs to be massive to deter a potential U.S. attempted disarming counterforce first strike. Except for an extreme crisis, when the United States would be already convinced that Moscow was imminently launching a strike (and thus would not be deterred by the size of the surviving forces), it is difficult or perhaps even impossible to imagine the circumstances under which a U.S. President would consider the risk of even one strategic warhead hitting one U.S. city to be worth the benefit of a preemptive strike. If this reality could be conveyed through a confidential bilateral exchange, it could provide a degree of reassurance.

CHAPTER SIX

Conclusion

Since the dawn of the nuclear age, the issue of preemptive strikes—how to negate their effectiveness by maintaining survivable forces and disincentivize them through arms control—has been central to both Washington's and Moscow's strategies and policies. In this report, we have evaluated a core paradox of the U.S.-Soviet/Russian bilateral dyad: Both define *stability* as confidence in the mutual ability to retaliate even after a preemptive strike, but, to varying degrees, both have developed capabilities that could limit the other's ability to retaliate. Particularly after the end of the Cold War, that variation grew wider as the United States maintained significant prompt counterforce capabilities while Russia focused on—and has become increasingly concerned about—its capacity to respond. Today, those concerns are the cause of significant instability.

As this report has demonstrated, current U.S. policy—specifically, maintaining significant prompt counterforce capabilities—came about for a variety of historically contingent reasons. It has endured, with some variation, for nearly half a century, despite dramatic changes in geopolitics and nuclear capabilities, including significant numerical reductions negotiated bilaterally with Moscow. Fundamentally changing U.S. policy seems highly unlikely as of this writing; path dependency aside, there are important unanswered—and unanswerable—questions about the consequences of such a change for U.S. national security.

However, we have also outlined several modest mutual self-restraint measures that could lessen the destabilizing effects of current policy. If successfully negotiated with Russia, these measures could provide greater stability both in peacetime and during a potential acute crisis. They would also not require a significant shift in current approaches to procurement, deployment, or employment. Although these measures, even taken together, will only chip away at the problem rather than resolve it completely, any costs associated with them would be modest. Barring an unforeseen opportunity to reconsider the fundamentals of U.S. nuclear strategy vis-à-vis Russia—specifically, the necessity of maintaining significant capabilities for prompt counterforce strikes—modest steps, such as the ones outlined in this report, could provide needed guardrails for U.S.-Russian strategic stability in a period when tensions in the bilateral relationship are likely to remain high.

Abbreviations

ABM	antiballistic missile
BMD	ballistic missile defense
CPGM	conventional precision-guided missile
ICBM	intercontinental ballistic missile
MIRV	multiple independently targetable reentry vehicle
MoD	Ministry of Defense
MT	megaton
NATO	North Atlantic Treaty Organization
NC3	nuclear command, control, and communication
NFU	no first use
NPR	Nuclear Posture Review
NSDM	National Security Decision Memorandum
NUWEP	Nuclear Weapons Employment Policy
SLBM	submarine-launched ballistic missile
SSBN	nuclear-powered ballistic missile submarine
START	strategic arms reduction treaty

References

Akhmerov, D. E., E. N. Akhmerov, and M. G. Valeev, "Uyazvimost' kontseptsii neyadernogo razoruzheniya strategicheskikh yadernykh sil Rossii," *Vestnik Akademii voennykh nauk*, No. 1, 2016, pp. 37–41.

Anderson, Justin, "Nuclear Weapons and the Laws of War (Cont.)," *Arms Control Wonk*, blog post, May 11, 2016. As of October 1, 2020: https://www.armscontrolwonk.com/archive/1201365/ nuclear-weapons-and-the-laws-of-war-cont/

Andryushin, I. A., A. K. Chernyshev, and Yu. A. Yudin, *Ukroshchenie yadra: Stranitsy istorii yadernogo oruzhiya i yadernoi infrastruktury SSSR*, Sarov, Russia: Tipografiya «Krasnyi Oktyabr'», 2003.

Anin [Antonov], Anatoly, "Vliyanie strategicheskikh nastupatel'nykh vooruzhenii v neyadernom osnashchenii na strategicheskuyu stabil'nost'," *Mirovaya ekonomika i mezhdunarodnye otnosheniya*, No. 6, 2011, pp. 45–55.

Anin [Antonov], Anatoly, "Pro Ssha—podryvayushchii doverie potentsial," *Mirovaya ekonomika i mezhdunarodnye otnosheniya*, No. 3, 2012, pp. 12–19.

Arbatov, Alexei G., and Vladimir Dvorkin, "The Impact of MIRVs and Counterforce Targeting on the U.S.-Russian Strategic Relationship," in Michael Krepon, Travis Wheeler, and Shane Mason, eds., *The Lure and Pitfalls of MIRVs: From the First to the Second Nuclear Age*, Washington, D.C.: Stimson Center, 2016, pp. 55–93.

Arbatov, Alexei G., Vladimir Z. Dvorkin, and Sergei K. Oznobishchev, eds., *Rossiya i dilemmy yadernogo razoruzheniya*, Moscow, Russia: Institute of World Economy and International Relations of the Russian Academy of Sciences, 2012.

Blair, Bruce G., "De-Alerting Strategic Nuclear Forces," in Harold A. Feiveson, ed., *The Nuclear Turning Point: A Blueprint for Deep Cuts and De-Alerting of Nuclear Weapons*, Washington, D.C.: Brookings Institution, 1999, pp. 101–127.

Blair, Bruce G., with Jessica Sleigh and Emma Clare Foley, *The End of Nuclear Warfighting: Moving to a Deterrence-Only Posture: An Alternative U.S. Nuclear Posture Review*, Princeton, N.J.: Program on Science and Global Security, Princeton University, 2018.

Boitsov, Markell, "Terminologiya v voennoi doktrine," *Nezavisimoe voennoe obozrenie*, October 31, 2014. As of October 1, 2020:
https://nvo.ng.ru/concepts/2014-10-31/10_doctrina.html

Brezkun, S. T., *Mech ili vesy? Yadernyi faktor v probleme voiny i mira*, Sarov, Russia: FGUP «RFYaTs-VNIIEF», 2016.

Brown, Seyom, "The New Nuclear MADness," *Survival*, Vol. 62, No. 1, 2020.

Buchan, Glenn, David M. Matonick, Calvin Shipbaugh, and Richard Mesic, *Future Roles of U.S. Nuclear Forces: Implications for U.S. Strategy*, Santa Monica, Calif.: RAND Corporation, MR-1231-AF, 2003. As of May 20, 2021:
https://www.rand.org/pubs/monograph_reports/MR1231.html

Burenok, V. M., and Yu. A. Pechatnov, "O kriterial'nykh osnovakh yadernogo sderzhivaniya," *Vooruzheniya i ekonomika*, No. 1, 2013, pp. 21–30.

Burr, William, "The 'Launch on Warning' Nuclear Strategy and Its Insider Critics," National Security Archive webpage, June 11, 2019. As of October 1, 2020:
https://nsarchive.gwu.edu/briefing-book/nuclear-vault/2019-06-11/
launch-warning-nuclear-strategy-its-insider-critics

Burutin, A. G., G. N. Vinokurov, V. M. Loborev, S. F. Pertsev, and Yu. A. Podkorytov, "Kontseptsiya nepriemlemogo ushcherba: genezis, osnovnye prichiny transformatsii, sovremennoe sostoyanie," *Vooruzhenie. Politika. Konversiya*, No. 4, 2010, pp. 3–8.

"D. Rogozin: SShA za pervye chasy voiny mogut unichtozhit' 90% raket RF," *RBK*, June 28, 2013.

Dunlap, Charles J., Jr., "Taming Shiva: Applying International Law to Nuclear Operations," *Air Force Law Review*, Vol. 42, 1997, pp. 157–171. As of October 1, 2020:
https://scholarship.law.duke.edu/cgi/
viewcontent.cgi?referer=&httpsredir=1&article=5202&context=faculty_scholarship

Dvorkin, Vladimir, and Aleksei Produkin, *Povest' o 4 TsNII MO i yadernoi sderzhivanii*, Yubileinyi, Russia: PTSM, 2009.

Enthoven, Alain C., and K. Wayne Smith, *How Much Is Enough? Shaping the Defense Program, 1961–1969*, New York: Harper & Row, 1971.

Freedman, Lawrence, and Jeffrey Michaels, *The Evolution of Nuclear Strategy*, 4th ed., New York: Palgrave Macmillan, 2019.

Gaddis, John, *Strategies of Containment: A Critical Appraisal of American National Security Policy During the Cold War*, New York: Oxford University Press, 2005.

Gaddis, John, "The Long Peace: Elements of Stability in the Postwar International System," *International Security*, Vol. 10, No. 4, Spring 1986, pp. 99–142.

Gavin, Francis J., *Nuclear Statecraft: History and Strategy in America's Atomic Age*, Ithaca, N.Y.: Cornell University Press, 2012.

Geist, Edward, *Armageddon Insurance: Civil Defense in the United States and Soviet Union, 1945–1991*, Chapel Hill, N.C.: University of North Carolina Press, 2019.

Geist, Edward, and Dara Massicot, "Understanding Putin's Nuclear 'Superweapons,'" *SAIS Review of International Affairs*, Vol. 39, No. 2, 2019, pp. 103–117.

Glaser, Charles L., *Analyzing Strategic Nuclear Policy*, Princeton, N.J.: Princeton University Press, 1990.

Glaser, Charles L., and Steve Fetter, "Should the United States Reject MAD? Damage Limitation and U.S. Nuclear Strategy Toward China," *International Security*, Vol. 41, No. 1, Summer 2016, pp. 49–98.

Green, Brendan Rittenhouse, and Austin Long, "The MAD Who Wasn't There: Soviet Reactions to the Late Cold War Nuclear Balance," *Security Studies*, Vol. 26, No. 4, 2017, pp. 606–641.

Gronlund, Lisbeth, and David C. Wright, "Depressed Trajectory SLBMs: A Technical Evaluation and Arms Control Possibilities," *Science & Global Security*, Vol. 3, Nos. 1–2, 1992, pp. 101–159.

Harvey, John R., "Assessing the Risks of a Nuclear 'No First Use' Policy," *War on the Rocks*, July 5, 2019. As of July 28, 2020:
https://warontherocks.com/2019/07/assessing-the-risks-of-a-nuclear-no-first-use-policy/

Hersman, Rebecca, William Caplan, and Bert Thompson, "Bad Idea: De-Alert U.S. ICBMs," *Defense360*, December 14, 2017. As of October 1, 2020:
https://defense360.csis.org/bad-idea-de-alert-u-s-icbms/

Hines, John, Ellis M. Mishulovich, and John F. Shulle, *Soviet Intentions 1965–1985*, Vol. 1, *An Analytical Comparison of U.S.-Soviet Assessments During the Cold War*, McLean, Va.: BDM Federal, 1995.

Jervis, Robert, *The Illogic of American Nuclear Strategy*, Ithaca, N.Y.: Cornell University Press, 1985.

Kahn, Hermann, *On Thermonuclear War*, Princeton, N.J.: Princeton University Press, 1960.

Kaplan, Fred, *The Wizards of Armageddon*, New York: Simon and Schuster, 1983.

Kaplan, Fred, *The Bomb*, New York: Simon & Schuster, 2020.

Kaplan, Lawrence, Ronald Landa, and Edward Drea, *The McNamara Ascendancy, 1961–1965*, Washington, D.C.: U.S. Government Printing Office, 2006.

Kaufmann, William, *The McNamara Strategy*, New York: Harper & Row, 1964.

Kofman, Michael, Anya Fink, and Jeffrey Edmonds, *Russian Strategy for Escalation Management: Evolution of Key Concepts*, Washington, D.C.: CNA, April 2020.

Kokoshin, A. A., "Asimmetrichnyi otvet nomer odin," *Nezavisimoe voennoe obozrenie*, July 27, 2007. As of October 3, 2019:
http://nvo.ng.ru/concepts/2007-07-27/4_otvet.html

Kokoshin, A. A., ed., *Vliyanie tekhnologicheskikh faktorov na parametry ugroz natsional'noi i mezhdunarodnoi bezopasnosti, voennykh konfliktov i strategicheskoi stabil'nosti*, Moscow, Russia: Izdatel'stvo MGU, 2017.

Kovalev, V. I., "Yadernoe oruzhie i sreda bezopasnosti Rossii v XXI veke," *Strategicheskaya stabil'nost'*, No. 3, 2014, pp. 14–22.

Kozyulin, Vadim, "Soedinennye Shtaty na puti k strategicheskoi neuyazvimosti," Russian International Affairs Council webpage, July 1, 2020. As of October 1, 2020:
https://russiancouncil.ru/analytics-and-comments/analytics/
soedinennye-shtaty-na-puti-k-strategicheskoy-neuyazvimosti/

Krasnoslobodtsev, V. P., A. V. Raskin, S. S. Savel'ev, and O. S. Kupach, "Analiz vozmozhnosti po realizatsii SShA kontseptsii bystrogo global'nogo udara," *Strategicheskaya stabil'nost'*, No. 2, 2014, pp. 67–79.

Krepon, Michael, and Travis Wheeler, "Introduction," *The Lure and Pitfalls of MIRVs: From the First to the Second Nuclear Age*, Washington, D.C.: Stimson Center, 2016, pp. 13–17.

Kristensen, Hans M., and Matt Korda, "Russian Nuclear Forces, 2020," *Bulletin of the Atomic Scientists*, Vol. 76, No. 2, 2020b.

Kristensen, Hans M., and Matt Korda, "United States Nuclear Forces, 2020," *Bulletin of the Atomic Scientists*, Vol. 76, No. 1, 2020b, pp. 46–60.

Kristensen, Hans M., Robert S. Norris, and Ivan Oelrich, *From Counterforce to Minimal Deterrence: A New Nuclear Policy on the Path Toward Eliminating Nuclear Weapons*, Washington, D.C.: Federation of American Scientists and The Natural Resources Defense Council, Occasional Paper No. 7, April 2009.

Lewis, Jeffrey, "Minimum Deterrence," *Bulletin of the Atomic Scientists*, Vol. 64, No. 3, July/August 2008, pp. 38–41.

Lieber, Keir A., and Daryl G. Press, "The New Era of Counterforce: Technological Change and the Future of Nuclear Deterrence," *International Security*, Vol. 41, No. 4, Spring 2017, pp. 9–49.

Lilly, Bilyana, *Russian Foreign Policy Toward Missile Defense: Actors, Motivations, and Influence*, Washington, D.C.: Lexington Books, 2014.

Long, Austin, *Deterrence—From Cold War to Long War: Lessons from Six Decades of RAND Research*, Santa Monica, Calif.: RAND Corporation, MG-636-OSD/AF, 2008. As of May 21, 2021:
https://www.rand.org/pubs/monographs/MG636.html

Long, Austin, "Red Glare: The Origin and Implications of Russia's 'New' Nuclear Weapons," *War on the Rocks*, March 26, 2018. As of October 1, 2020:
https://warontherocks.com/2018/03/
red-glare-the-origin-and-implications-of-russias-new-nuclear-weapons/

Long, Austin, and Brendan Rittenhouse Green, "Stalking the Secure Second Strike: Intelligence, Counterforce, and Nuclear Strategy," *Journal of Strategic Studies*, Vol. 38, Nos. 1–2, 2015, pp. 38–73.

Mazarr, Michael J., "Beyond Counterforce," *Comparative Strategy*, Vol. 9, No. 2, 1990, pp. 147–162.

McDonnell, Timothy P., *"Diplomatic Wallop": Nixon and the Return of Counterforce*, Cambridge, Mass.: Massachusetts Institute of Technology, Political Science Department Research Paper No. 2018-3, April 6, 2018. As of October 1, 2020:
https://ssrn.com/abstract=3157775

Miles, Aaron R., *Implementing the Hedge Strategy in the 2018 Nuclear Posture Review*, Livermore, Calif.: Lawrence Livermore National Laboratory Center for Global Security Research, January 17, 2019. As of October 1, 2020:
https://cgsr.llnl.gov/content/assets/docs/NPR_hedge_planning_final.pdf

Mosher, David E., Lowell H. Schwartz, David R. Howell, and Lynn E. Davis, *Beyond the Nuclear Shadow: A Phased Approach for Improving Nuclear Safety and U.S-Russian Relations*, Santa Monica, Calif.: RAND Corporation, MR-1666-NSRD, 2003. As of December 2, 2020:
https://www.rand.org/pubs/monograph_reports/MR1666.html

Mozzhorin, Yu., *Tak eto bylo: Memuary Yu. A. Mozzhorina*, Moscow, Russia: ZAO Mezhdunarodnaya Programma Obrazovaniya, 2000.

National Security Council, "Policy for Planning the Employment of Nuclear Weapons," National Security Decision Memorandum 242, to Secretary of State; Secretary of Defense; Director, Central Intelligence Agency; and Director, Arms Control and Disarmament Agency, January 17, 1974. As of May 20, 2021:
https://fas.org/irp/offdocs/nsdm-nixon/nsdm_242.pdf

Office of General Counsel, *Department of Defense Law of War Manual*, Washington, D.C.: U.S. Department of Defense, June 2015. As of October 1, 2020:
https://archive.defense.gov/pubs/law-of-war-manual-june-2015.pdf

Office of Inspector General, *Evaluation of Nuclear Ballistic Missile Submarine (SSBN) Sustainment*, Washington, D.C.: U.S. Department of Defense, June 15, 2018. As of October 1, 2020:
https://media.defense.gov/2018/Jun/28/2001937172/-1/-1/1/
DODIG-2018-127.PDF

Panda, Ankit, "'No First Use' and Nuclear Weapons," Council on Foreign Relations webpage, backgrounder, July 17, 2018. As of July 28, 2020: https://www.cfr.org/backgrounder/no-first-use-and-nuclear-weapons

Payne, Keith B., "Strategic Hubris," in "Forum: The Case for No First Use: An Exchange," *Survival*, Vol. 51, No. 5, October–November 2009, pp. 28–31.

Payne, Keith B., and James Schlesinger, "Minimum Deterrence: Examining the Evidence," *Comparative Strategy*, Vol. 33, No. 1, February 2014.

Pechatnov, Yu. A., "Analiz otechestvennykh i zarubezhnykh podkhodov k formirovaniyu kontseptsii i mekhanizma sderzhivaniya ot razvyazyvaniya voennoi agressii," *Vooruzheniya i ekonomika*, No. 3, 2010.

Pechatnov, Yu. A., "Teoriya sderzhivaniya: genezis," *Vooruzheniya i ekonomika*, No. 2, 2016.

Pifer, Steven, *Missile Defense in Europe: Cooperation or Contention?* Washington, D.C.: Brookings Institution Arms Control Series Paper #8, May 2012.

PIR-Tsentr, "Yadernyi ushcherb," Yadernoe nerasprostranenine: Kratkaya entsiklopediya, undated. As of October 17, 2019: http://www.pircenter.org/sections/247-yadernyj-uscherb

Podvig, Pavel, "Russia and Military Uses of Space," in Pavel Podvig and Hui Zhang, eds., *Russian and Chinese Responses to U.S. Military Plans in Space*, Cambridge, Mass.: American Academy of Arts and Sciences, 2008. As of October 1, 2020: https://www.amacad.org/publication/russian-and-chinese-responses-us-military-plans-space/section/3

Podvig, Pavel, "The Window of Vulnerability That Wasn't: Soviet Military Buildup in the 1970s—A Research Note," *International Security*, Vol. 33, No. 1, Summer 2008, pp. 118–138.

Poznikhir, Viktor, speech given at the 8th Moscow International Security Conference, April 23, 2019. As of October 1, 2020: http://mil.ru/mcis/news/more.htm?id=12120794@cmsArticle

President of Russia, Voennaya doktrina Rossiiskoi Federatsii, February 5, 2010. As of October 1, 2020: http://kremlin.ru/supplement/461

President of Russia, "Poslanie prezidenta federal'nomu sobraniyu," March 1, 2018. As of October 1, 2020: http://www.kremlin.ru/events/president/news/56957

President of Russia, "Interview with Al Arabiya, Sky News Arabia and RT Arabic," October 13, 2019. As of October 17, 2019: http://en.kremlin.ru/events/president/news/61792

Pronin, Aleksandr, "Gonka za global'nym prevoskhodstvom," *Rossiiskoe Voennoe Obozrenie*, No. 4, April 2013, pp. 55–58.

"Putin: Rossii nel'zya isklyuchat' opasnost' naneseniya obezoruzhivayushchego udara," *Vzglyad*, June 19, 2013. As of October 1, 2020:
https://vz.ru/news/2013/6/19/637894.html

Ramoshkina, N. P., "Shirokomashtabnaya PRO SShA: Na puti k sozdaniyu 'pol'notsennoi' protivoraketnoi oborony," *Strategicheskaya stabil'nost'*, No. 2, 2018, pp. 12–21.

Ravenal, Earl C., "Counterforce and Alliance: The Ultimate Connection," *International Security*, Vol. 6, No. 4, Spring 1982, pp. 26–43.

Richard, Theodore, "Nuclear Weapons Targeting: The Evolution of Law and U.S. Policy," *Military Law Review*, Vol. 224, No. 4, 2016, pp. 862–974.

Rogov, S., V. Esin, and P. Zolotarev, "Eksperty predlagayut kompleks mer doveriya po strategicheskim vooruzheniyam," *Nezavisimoe voennoe obozrenie*, July 2, 2004.

Rogov, S., V. Esin, and P. Zolotaryov, "O kachestvennoi transformatsii rossiisko-amerikanskikh otnoshenii v strategicheskoi oblasti," *Rossiiskii sovet po mezhdunarodnym delam (RSMD) Rabochaya tetrad'*, No. 7, 2013.

Rogov, S., P. Zolotarev, V. Kuznetsov, and V. Esin, "Strategicheskaya stabil'nost' i yadernoe razoruzhenie v XXI veke," *Nezavisimoe voennoe obozrenie*, November 16, 2012.

Russian Ministry of Defense, "Nepriemlemyi ushcherb," webpage, undated. As of October 1, 2020:
http://dictionary.mil.ru/dictionary/Terminy-RVSN/item/141687/

Sagan, Scott D., "The Case for No First Use," *Survival*, Vol. 51, No. 3, 2009, pp. 163–182.

"SALT II and the Growth of Mistrust: Conference #2 of the Carter-Brezhnev Project: A Conference of U.S. and Russian Policymakers and Scholars Held at Musgrove Plantation, St. Simons Island, Georgia 6–9 May 1994," transcript, excerpt of May 7, Morning Session, National Security Archive, undated. As of October 1, 2020:
https://nsarchive2.gwu.edu//nukevault/ebb285/doc03.PDF

Shapley, Deborah, *Promise and Power: The Life and Times of Robert McNamara*, Boston: Little, Brown and Company, 1993.

Siver, S. V., V. D. Roldugin, and N. N. Tatsyshin, "Metodicheskii podkhod k analizu boevoi ustoichivosti perspektivnoi gruppirovki RVSN v usloviyakh vliyaniya faktorov neopredelennogo kharaktera," *Strategicheskaya stabil'nost'*, No. 3, 2018, pp. 22–25.

Sterlin, A. E., A. A. Protasov, and S. V. Kreidin, "Sovremennye kontseptsii i silovykh instrumentov strategicheskogo sderzhivaniya," *Voennaya mysl'*, No. 8, 2019. As of October 17, 2019:
https://vm.ric.mil.ru/Stati/item/203864/

Terriff, Terry, *The Nixon Administration and the Making of U.S. Nuclear Strategy*, Ithaca, N.Y.: Cornell University Press, 1996.

Tetrais, Bruno, "The Trouble with No First Use," in "Forum: The Case for No First Use: An Exchange," *Survival*, Vol. 51, No. 5, October–November 2009, pp. 23–26.

Tomilenko, Ekaterina, "Opasnym kursom," *Krasnaya zvezda*, October 11, 2016. As of October 1, 2020:
http://archive.redstar.ru/index.php/component/k2/item/30774-opasnym-kursom

United States and Soviet Union, Soviet-United States Joint Statement on Future Negotiations on Nuclear and Space Arms and Further Enhancing Strategic Stability, June 1, 1990, George H. W. Bush Presidential Library website, undated. As of October 1, 2020:
https://bush41library.tamu.edu/archives/public-papers/1938

U.S. Department of Defense, *Nuclear Posture Review Report*, April 2010. As of October 1, 2010:
https://dod.defense.gov/Portals/1/features/defenseReviews/NPR/2010_Nuclear_Posture_Review_Report.pdf

U.S. Department of Defense, *Report on Nuclear Employment Strategy of the United States Specified in Section 491 of 10 U.S.C.*, Washington, D.C., June 12, 2013. As of October 1, 2020:
http://fas.org/man/eprint/employ.pdf

U.S. Department of Defense, *Nuclear Posture Review 2018*, Washington, D.C., February 2018. As of May 4, 2020:
https://media.defense.gov/2018/Feb/02/2001872886/-1/-1/1/2018-NUCLEAR-POSTURE-REVIEW-FINAL-REPORT.PDF

U.S. Department of State, Written Statement of the Government of the United States of America Before the International Court of Justice, June 10, 1994. As of October 1, 2020:
https://www.icj-cij.org/public/files/case-related/93/8770.pdf

U.S. Department of State, "New START Treaty Aggregate Numbers of Strategic Offensive Arms," fact sheet, December 1, 2020

"V Genshtabe rasskazali o tselyakh sozdaniya amerikanskoi sistemy PRO," RIA-Novosti, April 24, 2019. As of October 1, 2020:
https://ria.ru/20190424/1553009169.html?in=t

Wolfe, Johnny, "Statement of Vice Admiral Johnny Wolf, USN, Director, Strategic Systems Programs, on FY 2022 Budget Request for Nuclear Forces and Atomic Energy Defense Activities," before the Subcommittee on Strategic Forces of the Senate Armed Services Committee, Washington, D.C., May 12, 2021.